ACCESS AMERICA
GUIDE TO THE
SOUTHWESTERN NATIONAL PARKS

An Atlas and Guide for Visitors with Disabilities

NORTHERN CARTOGRAPHIC

WEIDENFELD & NICOLSON
New York

Copyright © 1988, 1989 by Northern Cartographic

Published by Weidenfeld & Nicolson, New York
A Division of Wheatland Corporation
841 Broadway
New York, New York 10003-4793

Published in Canada by General Publishing Company, Ltd.

The phrase "Access America" is the trademarked slogan of the United States Architectural and Transportation Barriers Compliance Board (ATBCB). The publisher wishes to disclaim any relationship or affiliation with this federal agency. The use of this trademarked phrase, in the title of the publication, does not indicate or imply any endorsement of this publication or its information by this federal agency.

Library of Congress Cataloging-in-Publication Data

Access America guide to the southwestern national parks.

    1. National parks and reserves—Southwest, New—Guidebooks.   2. Southwest, New—Description and travel—1981–—Guide-books.   3. Parks and the handicapped—Southwest, New.   4. Handicapped—Travel—Southwest, New—Guidebooks.   I. Northern Cartographic, Inc.
E160.A28   1989   917.8   89-9126
ISBN 1-55584-402-2

Printed in Italy by New Interlitho S.p.A. - Milan
This book is printed on acid-free paper
First Edition
10 9 8 7 6 5 4 3 2 1

Also available: *Access America Guide to the Eastern National Parks, Access America Guide to the Rocky Mountain National Parks, Access America Guide to the Western National Parks.*

Table of Contents

Legend

Highways

═══════🛡75══════	Interstate Highway
────180────	U.S. Highway
────16────	State Highway
────89────	
– – – – – – – –	Gravel or Dirt Road

Road Elevations

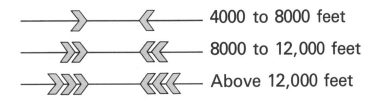

————————→———≪——— 4000 to 8000 feet

————————≫———≪≪——— 8000 to 12,000 feet

————————≫≫———≪≪≪——— Above 12,000 feet

The following symbols appear on the **Medical and Support Services** maps.

H	Hospital
W	Wheelchair Sales or Repair
P	Prosthetics and Orthotics
O	Therapeutic Oxygen
D	Dialysis
V	Veterinarian
GRAND JUNCTION	A city which offers all six services listed above.

The following symbols represent park places, facilities and features in the National Parks. Color represents the level of accessibility.

▨	Accessible
▢	Usable, Accessible with Assistance or Reported to be Accessible
◼	Not Accessible

Museum / Museum / **Museum**	Name of Place
🚺 🚺 🚺	Restroom, Women
🚹 🚹 🚹	Restroom, Men
R R R	Restrooms (park map)
⛲ ⛲ ⛲	Water
☎ ☎ ☎	Telephone
V V V	Vista
T T T	Picnic Table
S S S	Self-Guiding Trail
◣ ◣ ◣	Trail
🔊 🔊 🔊	Amphitheater
➕ ➕ ➕	Clinic or Hospital
⛺ ⛺ ⛺	Campground
♿ ♿ ♿	Parking
❓ ❓ ❓	Information
•••••••••	Route of Travel

▢	Administrative or Personnel Areas in Visitor Centers.

For a complete explanation of symbols and terms, please refer to the introduction.

Foreword

Outdoor recreation experiences are one of life's highlights. For me, these experiences have always been a tremendous source of personal rejuvenation and refreshment. It is unfortunate that the potential for these experiences is, in general, more limited for persons with disabilities than for non-disabled persons. This situation holds true even in our national parks, those special places designated to be the shared heritage of all Americans.

Compounding the lack of actual access has been the lack of clear and accurate information about "accessibility." Many times I have telephoned sites or read guides that have labeled places "accessible," only to find when I arrived, that there were accessible parking spaces or an accessible toilet, but no way to enter the nature center or picnic area or campground, nothing available in large print, and no telecommunication device for deaf persons.

Although there is a long way to go before equal opportunity for people of all levels of ability is achieved, things are changing. The national parks, in particular, have been responsive to the growing recognition of this need.

It was only several months ago that I was pleased to write the foreword to the award-winning parent publication of these Access America guides. Since that time, Access America: An Atlas and Guide to the National Parks for Visitors with Disabilities has become the object of much critical acclaim and has seen wide distribution to libraries and professional organizations around the country. It is a very exciting prospect that regional selections from that unique reference will now be available at the local bookstore in this Access America Guide Series.

The authors of Access America have demonstrated a remarkable awareness and understanding of the difficulties, both natural and man-made, faced by persons with disabilities. The final product is a testament to the rigorous process, including extensive surveys and site visits, employed to develop this series and the many years spent laying its groundwork.

Fifteen years ago the majority of accessible features described in these guides did not exist. The fact that progress has been made means that persons with disabilities have gained and are continuing to gain access to more opportunities.

I believe that all Americans, whether disabled or not, have the right to experience recreation and have access to recreation facilities and spaces. I commend the National Park Service for its initiatives to make the out-of-doors accessible to persons with disabilities.

I applaud the efforts of Northern Cartographic, Inc. to create a resource that will greatly enhance the outdoor recreation experiences of persons with disabilities and their families and friends. The interest, curiosity, and commitment demonstrated by the authors are exemplary.

Lex Frieden
Executive Director, TIRR Foundation, and
Assistant Professor, Baylor College of Medicine

Preface

Welcome to the *Access America Guide Series* on the national parks. It is our highest hope that the use of this long overdue and, in most respects, unique guide and atlas series will substantially enrich your next visit to some of our country's most treasured resources.

The concept of an atlas/guide to the national parks, specifically designed for visitors with disabilities, occurred in 1983. The idea took root in our professional backgrounds in geography and cartography as well as our personal travel experiences with family members. It was timely, coming in the midst of over a decade of progress in both attitudinal and physical changes which impacted directly on the "accessibility" of the parks themselves.

Communicating the nature and location of "access" is in large part a geographic statement and its ideal medium is *the map*. Although we felt well qualified to handle the graphic and technical aspects of the problems involved in this undertaking, a professional background in health and disability was conspicuously lacking. As the project evolved, this deficit was easily overcome.

Perhaps it was because of the inherent excitement of producing such an unparalleled atlas, or the generous spirit which characterizes many of the professionals in the health/disability field; whatever the reason, the five-hundred letters we sent out to recruit assistance with the project resulted in the creation of a talent pool of more than sixty individuals with backgrounds representing nearly all aspects of health and disability.

The response from the National Park Service was no less phenomenal. From our very first inquiry to the Park Service's Washington Office of Special Programs and Populations, through the myriad telephone calls to various Park Service agencies, to the numerous park personnel who labored through our intensive series of questionnaires, all greeted the idea with enthusiasm, energy and commitment.

The recent publication of our 464-page library reference, *Access America: An Atlas and Guide to the National Parks for Visitors with Disabilities*, culminated some five years of research and production, and has since received much critical acclaim. The travel series, now in hand, is based on a selected regional breakdown of this larger publication and fulfills our original committment to make this information available beyond the confines of libraries and professional organizations.

If we have succeeded in the purposes of producing these much needed guides, it is because of the generosity and cooperative efforts of hundreds of individuals, including many park visitors with disabilities, whose intellectual and material contributions have made this series a reality.

For all these people and for Northern Cartographic,

Peter Shea, Edward Antczak, Laura Feaster

Burlington, Vermont

Acknowledgments

Although Northern Cartographic claims exclusive responsibility for the nature, content and format of this atlas series (including any shortcomings), we have had considerable assistance in its research and production. The authors wish to acknowledge a number of individuals who gave generously and without reservation of their time, effort and expertise in the service of this project. It is no exaggeration to say that without their input completion of this series would have been impossible. Included in this group of exceptional people are: **Kay Ellis**, Recreation Specialist, National Park Service; **Franz Stillfried**, Information Coordinator/Advocate; **Steve Stone**, Access Coordinator, National Park Service; **Burt Wallrich**, Total Access Camping; **Erica Garfin**, Vermont Center for Independent Living; **Phyllis Cangemi**, Whole Access Project; **Meg Graf**, Spokes Unlimited.

Also **David Gaines**, National Park Service; **Nora Griffin-Shirley**, University of Arkansas at Little Rock; **Jim Tuck**, National Park Service; **Michael Warshawsky**, Access Advocate; **Ray Bloomer**, Disability Program Specialist, National Park Service; **Robert E. Michaels**, Arizona Bridge to Independent Living; **Ron Hanson**, Maine Governor's Committee on the Employment of the Handicapped; **Heidi Ann Johnson**, Ohio State University; **Jerry Duncan**, SCILL (Tours/Travel).

Also **Marianne J. Cashatt**, Woodrow Wilson Rehabilitation Center; **Robert M. Montague**, Special Olympics; **Colleen Trout** and **James Beck**, Challenge Alaska; **Helen Hecker**, Publisher/Writer; **Ray Cheever**, Accent on Living Magazine; **William G.B. Graham, M.D.**, University of Vermont; **Dale Brown**, National Network of Learning-Disabled Adults; **Mariam Brownson**, L.T.D. Travel; **Dolores A. Black**, Bowling Green State University.

Also **Peter Axelson**, Beneficial Designs; **Willie Cashin**, Woodrow Wilson Center for Independent Living; **Brent K. Askvig**, North Dakota Association for Persons with Severe Handicaps.

Although we are indebted to perhaps hundreds of individuals who in some fashion assisted us in our research, we are obliged to cite a number of contributors who were especially helpful in making this series a reality. They include: **John A. Nesbitt**, Special Recreation Inc.; **G. Andrew Fleming**, Paralyzed Veterans of America; **Dennis C. Almasy**, Access Specialist; **Dr.** and **Mrs. Samuel Genensky**, Center for the Partially Sighted; **Ruth Hall-Phillips**, Paralyzed Veterans of America; **Ismael S. Paredes**, California Governor's Committee for Employment of the Handicapped; **Chryss Jones**, Vermont Center for Independent Living; **Dr. Diana Richardson**, University of Maryland.

Also **Robert S. Zywicki**, The Itinerary Magazine; **Dr. Ronald J. Anderson**, University of Northern Iowa; **Gary W. Olsen**, National Association of the Deaf; **Merton J. Gilliam**, Rehabilitation Services Administration, Government of the District of Columbia; **Alton Hodges**, National Institute of Handicapped Research; **Ann Bowman**, National Park Service; **Nina M. Hill**, International Center for the Disabled.

Also **John Kopchik Jr.**, Disabled Outdoors; **Sharon Schleich**, Flying Wheels Travel; **Vicki Cook**, Goodwill Rehabilitation Inc.; **Barry Corbet**, Access Inc.; **Frank J. Deckert**, National Park Service; **Judith M. Dixon**, National Library Service for the Blind and Physically Handicapped.

Also **Robert Gorski**, President's Committee on the Employment of the Handicapped; **Marge Hadley**, Michigan Chapter, National Arthritis Foundation; **Dennis L. Heath**, State of Oregon; **Rosemarie Kasper**, Vocational Rehabilitation Counselor; **Robert B. Kasparek**, National Park Service; **Fred Marcus**, national park visitor; **E.C. Keller**, Foundation for Science and the Handicapped.

Also **Stuart R. Mace**, National Easter Seal Society; **Lorraine Marchi**, National Association for the Visually Handicapped; **Roberta Stein**, Barrier Free Alaska; and, **Syd Jacobs**, national park visitor.

National Park Service

For general support and research assistance we would like to thank David C. Park, Chief, and Thomas Coleman, Recreation Specialist, Special Programs and Populations Branch; David E. Gackenbach, Chief, Concessions Division; Warren H. Hill, Associate Regional Director of Operations, Midwest Region; Jody Notch, Technical Information Assistant, Denver Service Center; Edie Ramey, Chief, Technical Information Center, Denver Service Center; Ann Wazenski, Special Programs and Populations Branch; and, Ricardo Lewis, Public Relations.

We are deeply indebted to all the park personnel who took direct responsibility for responding to our lengthy and tedious questionnaires, and subsequently reviewing the text. These include: **Donald Fiero**, Chief of Interpretation and **Betty Romero**, Clerk, Mesa Verde N.P.; **David Karaszewski**, Zion N.P.; **Sandra H. Key**, Superintendent, Bryce Canyon N.P.; **Peter L. Parry**, Superintendent, Arches and Canyonlands N.P.'s, and **Jerry Rumburg**, Chief of Interpretation, Canyonlands N.P.; **Bill Gleason**, Accessibility Coordinator, Capitol Reef N.P.; **Karen Berggren**, Park Coordinator, **Paula Rooney**, Supervisor and **Kelly Martin**, Park Ranger, Grand Canyon N.P.; and, **Terry Maze**, Special Populations Coordinator, Petrified Forest N.P.

National Park Superintendents

We wish to acknowledge the enthusiastic and committed cooperation we received from the individual park superintendents. Their strong support of our efforts allowed full, active participation by the staff they supervise. Our gratitude is extended to Richard Marks, Grand Canyon N.P.; Edward Gastellum, Petrified Forest N.P.; Robert Heyder, Mesa Verde N.P.; Sherma Bierhaus, Arches N.P., Sandra Hellickson, Bryce Canyon N.P.; Peter Parry, Canyonlands N.P.; Robert Reynolds, Capitol Reef N.P.; and Harold Grafe, Zion N.P.

Introduction

Text Information

General

Someone once said, "Believe half of what you read . . ." Although the editors have made every effort to impart a considerably higher percentage of accuracy to the information which follows, the spirit of this proverbial dictum should pervade the use of this guidebook. Having a disability may make the visitor more vulnerable to the consequences of misinformation than would be the case with the non-disabled traveler; more care is therefore warranted. Park visitors with a disability must use this book not as the final step in their research and planning of a park visit, but as a good first step—a first step that leads to questions and follow-up at the level of the local park. If this book accompanies the visitor to the park, it should not be used as the exclusive source of accessibility information but as a basis of further inquiry to confirm, clarify and particularize each situation. Changes occur and mistakes get made; there is no substitute for vigilance. Through correspondence, telephone calls and on-the-spot interrogation of National Park Service personnel, visitors must judge their own personal abilities in relation to each feature and offering of an individual park. **The publisher and the authors disclaim completely any liability resulting from the use of any information contained in this publication.**

The idea of making critical comparisons among the parks included in this atlas/guide was resisted for a number of reasons. Foremost was the concern that by attempting to rate one park as more accessible than another the authors would be assuming a responsibility that is best left to the individual visitor. An evaluation would have required either a good deal of subjective judgement or a rather elaborate, objective "scoring" system that in the end may not have been meaningful at all. The parks themselves differ in size, degree of cultural development (number of buildings, trails and other amenities) as well as the number of program offerings. Each reader and would-be visitor will have different accessibility requirements and different personal interests. As a result, the accessibility of the parks tend to defy direct comparisons. We have therefore left it to the reader, according to their interests and tastes, to draw their own conclusions.

Research Methods

Before embarking on an exposition of the important categories of information incorporated in the text, a background in the method of the research and its research tools will aid the user in its interpretation.

The bulk of the access information was obtained by questionnaires submitted to the selected parks, and private concessionaires serving these parks.

In devising questionnaires, the authors balanced the requirement to produce useful, accurate information, with the need to limit the size of the questionnaires. A limitation on the size was necessary in order to make a response both inviting and feasible. Park staff are extremely busy and are currently operating under mandated budget cuts. Private concessions might perceive little immediate payback for investing time in responding. In the end, seven individualized questionnaires were designed and utilized. These questionnaires combined both standardized and open-ended questioning techniques. The questions were based in large part on accessibility standards known as UFAS, the Uniform Federal Accessibility Standards mandated by The Architectural Barriers Act of 1968, as amended. (A book detailing the Uniform Federal Accessibility Standards is available at a nominal charge from: Superintendent of Documents, U.S. Government Printing Office, Washington,

D.C. 20402.) For private concessions, the access standards of the American National Standards Institute (ANSI) were applied. Additional questions were added to ascertain certain features of program accessibility, and for areas not covered by UFAS, for example, "trails" and "campgrounds," accepted standards were applied analogously.

Three types of questionnaires were sent to the parks. The questions related specifically to 1) Programming (80 questions), 2) Visitor Centers (66 questions), and 3) Campgrounds (47 questions). In the cases of both visitor centers and campgrounds, multiple copies were furnished, one for each campground and visitor center. In all cases an effort was made to direct the questionnaires to those in-park National Park Service personnel who were most responsible for coordinating and promulgating "accessibility" for visitors with disabilities. The overall response rate from the parks was outstanding.

Questionnaires were also sent to private concessions. These concessions served the selected parks, and all were members of the Conference of National Park Concessions. Four types of questionnaires were employed, one for each type of concession: 1) Food and/or Lodging (164 questions), 2) Transportation (30 questions), 3) Mercantile (63 questions), and 4) Outdoor Experience/Adventure (15 questions). Where it was appropriate, multiple copies were furnished. In general, information for non-respondents is not included.

Access Rating

Based on questionnaire responses, the various park features, buildings, programs and private concessions were evaluated in relation to their accessibility. For general purposes, "access" refers the access requirements of a wheelchair user. The nature of "access" as it refers to other visitors—those with visual, hearing or developmental disabilities—is indicated by specific

description. For example, the statement that "The XYZ Film at the Visitor Center is accessible" refers only to access by wheelchair users. If there are additional access features of this program, such as film captioning or printed script, they are described specifically. Since the vast majority of access descriptions relate to the needs of visitors with mobility impairments, access information for visitors with visual, hearing or developmental disabilities has been highlighted by symbols in the margins to make them easier to identify.

"Accessible" or "fully accessible" means that a particular feature meets all or nearly all of the applicable access requirements as provided by the Uniform Federal Accessibility Standards. "Reported to be accessible" is a slightly downgraded version of "fully accessible." This rating was applied when information was furnished that indicated a feature was accessible, but that full, explanatory details were not provided on the questionnaire.

"Accessible with assistance" or "usable" applies to features which fail to meet one or more of the UFAS criteria but may still offer the potential for access by individuals who either have the help of a second party or might have the ability to use their wheelchair in an above-average or athletic manner. A smooth pathway with a steep gradient; a rough or sandy travel surface; a door requiring excessive force to open; a small, unbeveled change of level—all these might successfully be negotiated either with some assistance or exceptional skill, and therefore would have been given this classification. A flight of stairs would not.

"Not accessible" or "inaccessible" applies to features which, when they are judged against UFAS, may have multiple failings or a single, radical failure to meet standards. Some examples would include an access route to a visitor center which includes stairs, or a restroom with a door too narrow to admit a wheelchair user. Features and places rated "not accessible" may still be accessible to visitors with less severe mobility impairments, e.g., someone using a walker may be able to negotiate a set of stairs. Visitors with disabilities that are unrelated to mobility likely are capable of entering such facilities (with or without assistance) and must look to the text for particulars addressing their specific needs.

In most cases the text will contain detailed information describing any deviation from UFAS and will provide other relevant particulars.

Park Contact Office

The first information furnished concerning a park is the address and telephone number of that office within the park which is most directly responsible for addressing the needs of visitors with disabilities. In some cases this is the office of the Park Superintendent. In many cases, however, it is the "Accessibility Coordinator," "Special Populations Coordinator," "Public Information Officer" or similar office that is most prepared to provide the kinds of specialized information required.

Communication with this office should be a first priority in planning a visit, both to confirm and update the information found in this book and to pursue specific interests and needs. The parks are in continuous change, and given the current interest and momentum in "access," there is a good chance that additional accessibility will be available at the time of contact.

Depending on staff and available skills, some parks have the potential to pre-arrange special programming for visitors with disabilities. Where they occur, such possibilities are noted in the text. The office listed under this heading would be the most appropriate contact to initiate any of these arrangements.

Winter Visitation

This text section notes any factors that affect a winter visit. Some park facilities may be closed during the winter season; in others special considerations may apply.

Safety

This text section addresses personal safety considerations. If the subject matter were given an all-inclusive coverage, this short paragraph of text might have rambled for a score or more of pages for each park. As it stands, it simply highlights a few considerations deemed uniquely noteworthy for a particular park.

Elevation

A general statement concerning elevation of park roads is given in view of the fact that, because of its inverse relationship with available atmospheric oxygen, elevation has direct effects on physical stamina and cardiopulmonary function. (The atlas's park maps contain additional information on road elevations; the reader is directed to the map section under Elevation.)

Medical and Support Services

In-park clinics, if present, and the nearest hospitals are listed under this heading. Additional information is found in the Support Services maps. The nearest complete range of services is also noted. "Complete range of services" should be understood to mean the availability of: a licensed hospital, dialysis center (serving transients), retail wheelchair sales/repair, professional prosthetic and orthotic services, retail outlets for therapeutic oxygen and veterinarian services (for animal guides). Many communities may have one or more of these services available and be geographically closer to the park than those locations with a "complete range of services." See Support Services maps.

Publications

In this section National Park Service publications which have been produced *specifically* to inform visitors with disabilities are listed, along with information on how and where they may be obtained. If a park newspaper, or other publication written for general readership, contains specific access information, it is also noted.

Transportation

Some parks restrict the use of private vehicles within the park. Other parks maintain shuttle services for visitors, or license private concessions to offer transportation services. This section contains a general assessment of transportation within a park.

TDD

A statement on the availability of TDD communication for visitors with hearing disability is provided for each park.

Sign Language Interpreter

Some parks may have on staff personnel which are trained in American Sign Language (ASL), programs conducted in ASL, or emergency procedures for contacting a sign language interpreter. The availability of these services (at present they are rare) is noted in this section.

Dog Guides

Park policy concerning the use of dog guides, as well as any special consideration, is stated here.

Programs

This section is divided into organized programs and self-guided programs and it highlights their accessibility. Organized programs generally consist of films, campfire programs, ranger-led activities and scheduled events. Self-guided programs include such considerations as personal sightseeing, traveling on trails which are interpreted by signs or a printed brochure, picnicking, visiting museum displays and other types of activities in which the participant directs his or her schedule and course. Emphatically it is the visitor with mobility impairment who is addressed in this section. This is a direct reflection of the current nature of "access" at the parks; for although our questions attempted to achieve a more balanced picture, the responses emphasized access as it relates to visitors with mobility impairments.

Unless otherwise stated, "access" refers to access by a wheelchair user. Other types of access—taped or printed scripts, captioned films, tactile exhibits, program formats featuring simple pictures and explanations (for visitors with developmental disability), etc.—are stated specifically. To help the user identify programs with features of particular relevance to visitors with visual, hearing or developmental disability, margin keys will assist in locating appropriate information.

Visual Disability

Hearing Disability

Developmental Disability

Visitors with mobility-related disabilities will claim the greatest interest in the balance of the text, though the locations of general programs and available facilities would be of interest to all readers. Park locations set in **bold text** are represented on Park Maps or Insets.

Self-Guided Trails and Trails

Although in some cases the differences between self-guided trails and just "trails" are somewhat blurred, these sections contain information on all park trails that have been designed specifically for visitors with disabilities, trails that might be negotiated with assistance and, in rare cases, trails that coincidentally meet accessibility standards on grades, width and type of surface. Self-guided trails feature interpretive signs or are accompanied by a descriptive brochure; trails do not.

Exhibits

Highlighted in this section is accessibility to displays and exhibits maintained by the National Park Service or by cooperative agencies such as local historical and natural history associations.

Visitor Centers

Physical accessibility to the parks' visitor centers is described with respect to parking, path of travel to entrances, and interior facilities. The elements of the interior of visitor centers which were reviewed include the information counter, restroom, water fountain and public telephone service. The fact that this section is addressed *de facto* almost exclusively to wheelchair users, or visitors who are otherwise mobility impaired, reflects the existing situation. Aside from some occasional modifications to public telephones, physical modifications that consider visitors with hearing, visual or other disabilities are rare.

Campgrounds

Parks may designate and reserve a number of campsites for optional use by visitors with mobility impairments. Some of these sites have been designed specifically for wheelchair users and contain a number of modifications. Other designated sites simply represent camping locations which, when reviewed against all other available locations, offer the most potential for visitors using wheelchairs ("best" gradient, type of surface, proximity to restroom facilities, etc.) Park campgrounds included in this section are described in terms of their parking, paths of travel to campsite and other facilities, restrooms, sources of water, cooking grates·and other modifications.

Basic Facilities Chart

For reader convenience a chart summarizing a park's accessible restrooms, water fountains and telephones has been provided. (Access to wheelchair users only is considered.) Although this chart provides a quick overview of a park, the reader must refer to the details of the text in order to develop an accurate picture of the access features and requirements of a given location.

Supplementary Information

The focus of this section is the private concessions that serve the parks. Unless otherwise stated, information regarding the concessions was obtained from our own questionnaires. Several types of concessions are considered: lodging, food service, transportation, gift shops and other retail stores (groceries, camping supplies) and "adventure experiences."

Brief statements regarding accessibility of some concessions have been taken from published sources, notably the Second Edition of "National Parks Visitor Facilities and Services," published by the Conference of National Park Concessions. In the case of these concessions, the standards applied in assessing their accessibility are unknown to the editors. The reader, who should be routinely prudent in relying on any access information, should make detailed inquiries to these concessions about all aspects of accessibility.

Concessions offering "adventure experiences," such as whitewater rafting, horseback riding and mountain climbing, were asked different questions than the other concessions. The main difference was that the standardized questions about physical access were omitted. This was done under the assumption that the physical plant where the concession operates is inconsequential to the activity, also that the activity itself is inherently not "accessible." In these cases emphasis was given to the concessionaire's experience with and willingness to serve clients with disabilities.

Reading and Using the Maps

General Features

Recognizing that a certain percentage of the readers of this guide series would have less-than-optimum eyesight, the authors have put some effort into producing maps that could be easily read. This requirement was tempered only by the desire to avoid producing graphics that would appear grotesque or cartoon-like to the general readership. Although there is a body of research on the production of tactile maps for readers with profound visual impairment, there has been very little research on mapping for readers with partial vision. As a result, the cartographic design proceeded more by intuition than on a solid groundwork of successfully proven models. Its aim was to create maps that would be readable by a "visually mixed" audience.

"Accessibility" to the parks is described in part by a series of maps which highlight the information found in the park texts. (For a description of the criteria of accessibility, see the Access Information section.) Each series is executed at an increasingly larger scale, giving a progressively "closer look" at the pertinent information. Unless otherwise noted, as in the case of the visitor center diagrams, all the maps have a standard orientation, with North at the top.

Throughout this series of maps a continuity in color theme has been applied:

The color "BLUE" is associated with accessible features. Although the Uniform Federal Accessibility Standards (UFAS) were used as the general yardstick in evaluating access, a "blue" rating is not necessarily synonymous with a feature's meeting these standards. For example, in the case of the support services surrounding a park there was no evaluation of access whatsoever. (See below under Support Services.) In some cases, such as campgrounds, there are no legally applicable Uniform Federal Accessibility Standards. The editors were compelled to interpret individual situations creatively. There are other occurrences where access to a particular feature may have required a "judgment call." These judgments, however, were made discernedly and applied conservatively.

The color "RED" is associated with features which while failing to meet Uniform Federal Accessibility Standards, may be accessible with assistance, "usable," or otherwise offer some potential for access. In addition, there are a number of park features "reported to be accessible" but the specific details necessary to confirm their accessibility had not been supplied. These features have also been indicated in red.

The color "BLACK" is associated with features that are not accessible. (Black is also used for the labeling involved in general geographic orientation: names of places, mountains, rivers, boundaries, etc.)

Locator Maps

These maps are intended to provide an orientation to a park's location and include a generalized road network of the region. Park visitors should refer to standard road maps and atlases for their basic highway navigation.

Medical and Support Services Maps

The first class of maps to contain substantive access information is "Medical and Support Services." These maps portray a selection of important products and/or services that are available within approximately a 100-mile radius of each park. Sources for this information included the local "yellow pages," the rosters of professional organizations and a computer-generated printout based on a product's or a service's Standard Industrial Code and the geographically relevant zip codes. The types of products and services included are hospitals ("H"), retail outlets selling or repairing wheelchairs ("W"), retail outlets selling therapeutic oxygen ("O"), prosthetic and orthotic products and services

("P"), dialysis centers ("D") and veterinarians, for the clinical treatment of animal guides, ("V"). Pharmacies were not included because their occurrence is so common that there seemed little need to document them; also their omission produces less cluttered maps.

In some cities and larger towns, all six of these services are available, in which case the name of the locale itself is represented in blue, e.g. "MIDDLETOWN."

Symbols for all the services are represented in "BLUE." In regard to services, the focus is on their "availability" and not their "accessibility." In other words, access to the hospitals and to the stores selling or repairing wheelchairs, or orthotics, or therapeutic oxygen, etc. is not addressed, but given the nature of some of these specialties one would hope for reasonable accessibility to them.

For detailed information concerning the services indicated, the reader should inquire at the local level. A summary of the type of dialysis and related service offered by the various centers listed on the map is available from "The List," c/o Dialysis and Transplantation, 7628 Densmore Ave., Van Nuys, California 91406, telephone: (818) 782-7328. Information concerning the selected prosthetic and orthotic services can be obtained by writing or calling the American Orthotic and Prosthetic Association, 717 Pendleton Street, Alexandria, Virginia 22314, telephone: (703) 836-7116. Other services may be contacted by referring to the local yellow pages of the phone book of the city or town named on the map. (A local library may have a surprisingly large holding of phone books from around the country.)

Park Maps

In all cases it is recommended that the visitor obtain and use the official National Park Service map of the park they are visiting. These maps, which usually accompany admission to the park or which may be obtained by mail, will furnish more complete, more detailed travel and geographic information than the maps in this guide. By using the official park map in conjunction with the maps and information in this guide, the visitor will enhance the utility of both sources of information.

The park maps which follow focus on and highlight accessibility information using the blue-red-black color theme. Features included on the map are:

Visitor Centers (labeled by name)   ABC Visitor Center

Restroom Facilities   R

Drinking Water

Telephone

Medical Clinics

Amphitheaters

Campgrounds (labeled by name)   XYZ Campground

Picnic Areas

Scenic Vistas   V

Self-Guiding Trails   S

Trails

Where available a selection of private concessions is also represented (labeled by name), along with the facilities from the above list.

Elevation

As elevation increases, the amount of oxygen in the air decreases. This depletion has significant effects on a person's cardiovascular system; the heart and lungs must work harder to maintain the same level of oxygen, and muscles are more susceptible to exhaustion. These effects are quite noticeable, even to non-disabled people. For a person who expends considerable energy using a wheelchair or other ambulatory assists, and for those with cardiopulmonary health problems, these effects may be exaggerated. If there is any cause for concern for health risks, the prospective park visitor should consult a physician before venturing into the situation.

Persons with obstructive lung disease are particularly susceptible to the effects of elevation.

A statement regarding road elevations is positioned at the bottom of each park map. (The park text may also contain elevation information.) Changes in elevation, at 4000-foot intervals, are shown along park roads by means of orange chevrons. The chevrons always point *uphill*. The number of chevron bars indicates the level of elevation: one, above 4000 feet; two, above 8000 feet; three, above 12,000. (See map legend.)

Visitor Center Diagrams

Where available, schematic drawings of particular visitor centers have been included. The majority of these are based on architectural drawings and blueprints obtained from the National Park Service's Technical Information Center in Denver, Colorado. Some diagrams were based on blueprints or other drawings gleaned from the individual park's holdings. Others were based on hand-drawn sketches by knowledgeable park personnel. Still others represent a combination of a blueprint drawing supplemented by hand-drawn sketches with the addition of relevant outlying information not shown on the original blueprint. For this reason no map scale is provided with these diagrams. For travel distances the reader should refer to the text descriptions.

The reader should also note that the orientation of a Visitor Center Diagram may vary from the conventional, "North-at-the-top," standard. What has persuaded this deviation from the convention was the preference given to placing the main entrance "facing" the reader. Although for some diagrams, the cartographic liberties taken with the diagram orientations may require momentary patience on the part of the reader, all the diagrams contain sufficient information for successful orientation.

The blue-red-black color theme, as related to accessibility, is continued in this diagram series. As with the other maps, certain background information is presented in black. Such information may include building outlines, sidewalk locations, labeled features (e.g. "Main Entrance") and other orientational information. In such cases, the color is irrelevant to "access." If in doubt, the reader should refer to the text for clarification.

Arches

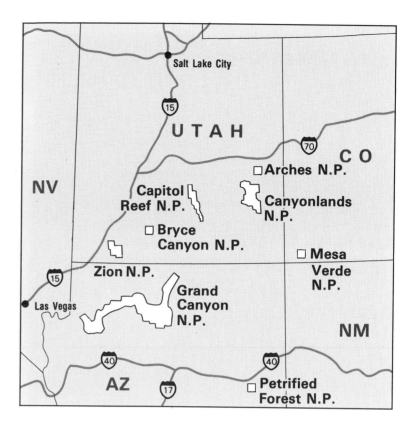

**Superintendent
National Park Service
Arches National Park
Moab, UT 84532
Tel. (801) 259-8161**

The impressive sculptured landscape of Arches National Park is located in southeastern Utah's red rock country. Spires and pinnacles reach up into the clear blue sky and rocks perch on seemingly inadequate bases. The famous arches seem like giant spectacles through which to view the surrounding natural beauty.

These features were created during the course of 100 million years of erosion by wind, water, extreme temperatures and underground salt movements. Alternating periods of freezing and thawing caused the porous sandstone to crumble, eventually leaving holes in narrow walls. Further weathering enlarged these holes to form arches. In contrast, natural bridges, which may look like arches, are formed in the paths of streams.

Arches National Park contains the greatest density of natural arches in the world. More than 500 arches are catalogued. The smallest arch has an opening of only three feet, while the largest one, called Landscape Arch, is over 100 feet high and nearly 300 feet across at the base. All stages of arch formation and decay are found here.

Sometimes illuminated at sunset, Fiery Furnace presents a dramatic view from Panorama Point or the Fiery Furnace Viewpoint. Visitors may also wish to travel to Wolfe Ranch, the remains of a ranch and old log cabin built in 1888.

This is semi-arid canyon country that is twenty-five percent exposed stone. Piñon pines and gnarled juniper trees add a splash of green contrast to the red sandstone. Colorful displays of wildflowers occur in spring when conditions are favorable. Wildflowers may be found blooming in and around moist places from May to August.

Most wildlife species here are nocturnal, but you may sight reptiles, jackrabbits, kangaroo rats or other small rodents. Lucky visitors may spot a mule deer or kit fox. Piñon jays, golden eagles and redtail hawks are some of the resident birds. Several other migratory species may also be seen.

Much of the untrampled desert area is covered with a fragile dark brown blanket called "cryptogamic soil." It is composed of several species of mosses, lichens, fungi and algae. This ground cover helps other vegetation become established by absorbing moisture, providing nutrients and preventing erosion.

Climate Chart

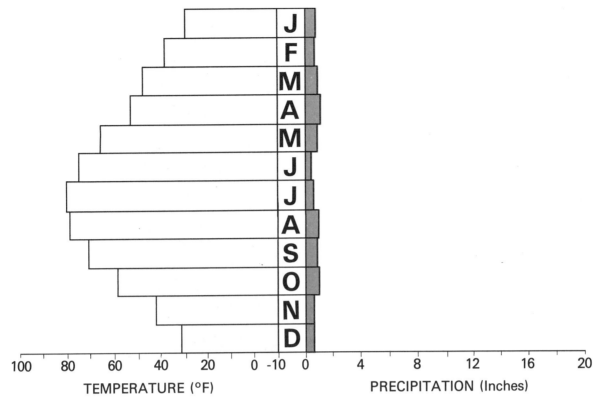

TEMPERATURE (°F)   PRECIPITATION (Inches)

Station Location: Moab, Utah
Station Elevation: 3965 feet

General Information

Weather

Summer daytime temperatures can reach 110°F. Spring and fall are generally warm with average temperatures ranging from the 40's to the low 60's. Winter temperatures are cold. Precipitation is sparse but uniformly distributed throughout the year. April is the wettest month, averaging almost two inches of rainfall.

Winter Visitation

The park is open during winter. The possibility of snow presents special considerations.

Elevation

The climate and landscape at Arches can cause dehydration and heat problems. The average elevation of main park features is 5000 feet. Visitors should caution against overexertion under these conditions.

Medical and Support Services

The nearest hospital is located in Moab, Utah, about five miles from the park entrance. A complete range of services can be found in Grand Junction, Colorado and Salt Lake City, Utah.

Publications

There are no publications available that directly address the needs of visitors with disabilities. Brochure information about the physical requirements and other aspects of specific park resources are available but limited.

Transportation

Private cars may be used for travel in the park.

Sign Language Interpreter

There are no interpreters with signing skills on the staff. Some seasonal employees may have signing abilities but may not be present from year to year.

Medical and Support Services

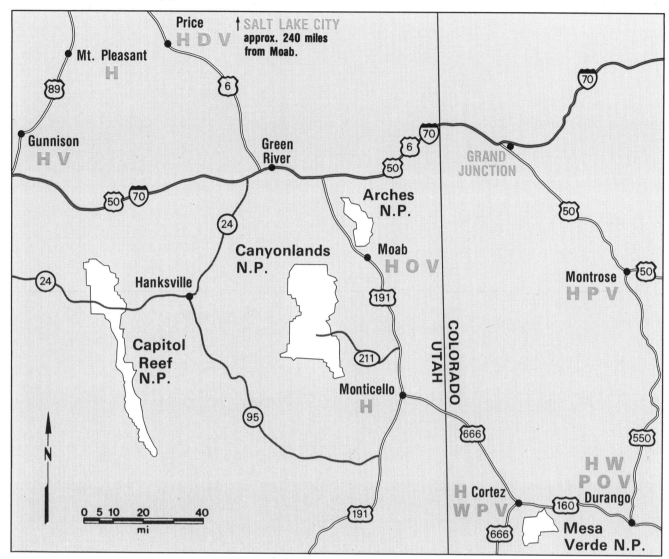

There are no pre-arrangements to contact an interpreter in the event of an emergency.

TDD

There is no TDD capability within the park.

Dog Guides

Dog guides are permitted in the park.

Programs

Organized Programs

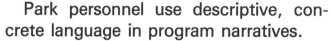 Park personnel use descriptive, concrete language in program narratives.

During programs, park personnel usually include items that may be touched.

Programs may be given at **Fiery Furnace, Devils Garden, Windows** or any-where the staff members wish to conduct one. Accessibility at individual program locations must be determined while in the park.

Special communication techniques may be used during program presentations for visitors with developmental disabilities in a group setting. There are limited personnel for these presentations. Special arrangements for such programs may not be possible. Inquire well in advance.

• Programs at the **Visitor Center** include a slide show. The Visitor Center is accessible with assistance (see *Visitor Center* section for details). Allowances have been made for wheelchair users in the program area.

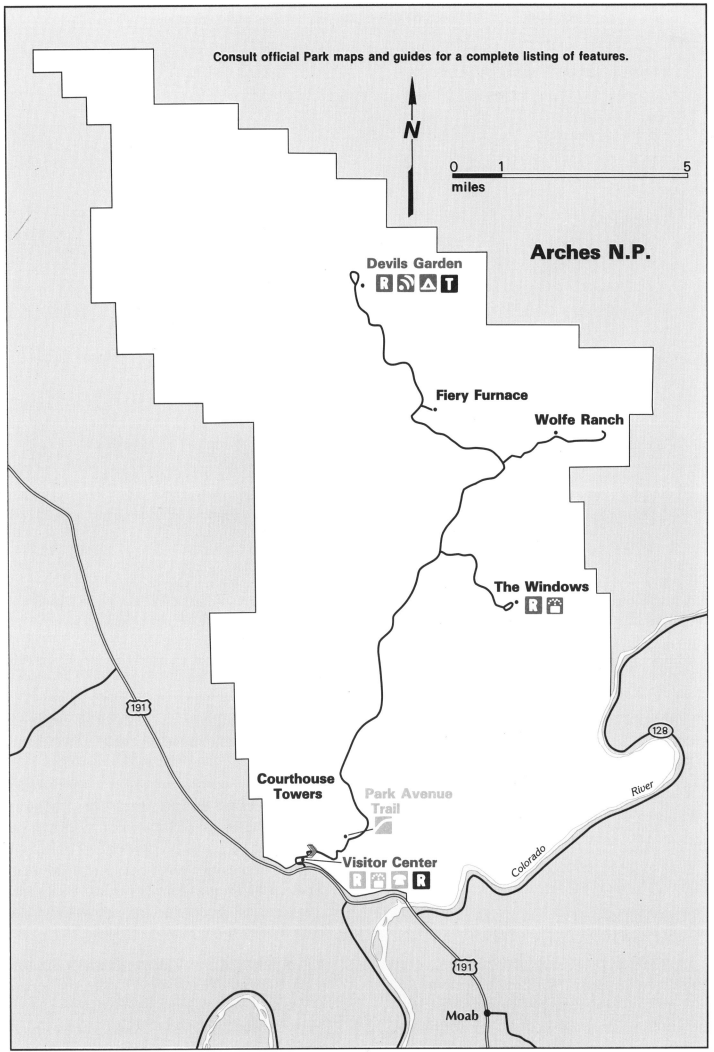

Consult official Park maps and guides for a complete listing of features.

N

0   1   5
miles

Arches N.P.

Devils Garden
R ⌇ ▲ T

Fiery Furnace

Wolfe Ranch

The Windows
R ⌂

Courthouse
Towers

Park Avenue
Trail

Visitor Center
R ⌂ ⌁ R

191

128

Colorado   River

191

Moab

Park roads range from just under 4000 to just under 6000 ft. in elevation.

USGS – J.R. GILL

Park Avenue resembles a city skyline.

• There is an evening program at **Devils Garden Campground Amphitheater.** It is reported to have accessible parking. Restrooms and water are not accessible to wheelchair users. Paths of travel from the parking area to the program area are concrete and are reported to be accessible. Allowances have been made for wheelchairs in the program area.

• A slide show and cards are available that portray some of the information from interpretive programs which wheelchair users cannot access.

Self-Guided Programs

• There is a self-guided program at the Museum.

• A self-guided auto tour of the park is available.

• There is no self-guiding material available in audio form.

Trails

• Park Avenue Trail is an interpretive trail specifically designed for visitors with mobility impairments. The trailhead is about two miles north of the **Visitor Center**. There is a sign at the trailhead relating pertinent information about the trail.

• The Desert Nature Trail at the **Visitor Center** does not meet UFAS.

• Trailheads at **The Windows** are reported to have accessible restrooms and water.

Exhibits

• Exhibit information is not available in audio, large-print or braille format.

• Adequate and even lighting is used to display exhibits.

• Tactile exhibits can be found at the **Visitor Center** and Museum.

• Interpretive signs may be either routed or raised.

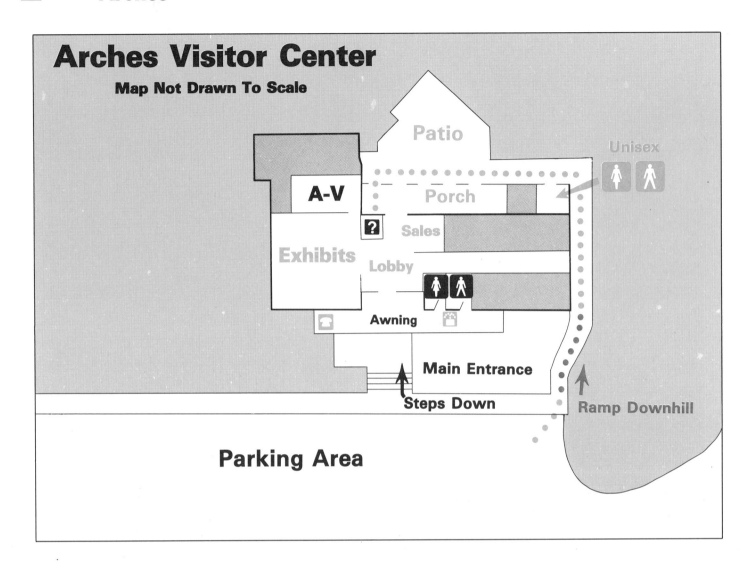

Visitor Centers

Note: Information about Arches National Park is available at Canyonlands National Park Headquarters Visitor Center in Moab, Utah. (See Canyonlands N.P. Visitor Centers section for accessibility.)

Visitor Center
• Located off U.S. Route 191 at the park entrance.
• There is reserved, signed, accessible parking about 150 feet from the Visitor Center. There is a passenger loading zone which is reported to be accessible. Necessary curb cuts are in place and the surface of the parking area is level and smooth.
• There is a continuous route from the reserved parking to the rear entrance. A ramp is in use on this route. Its rise was not specified, so assistance may be necessary. The ramp is equipped with handrails.

• The information desk is higher than 34 inches.
• A unisex restroom is reported to be fully accessible. The restroom entrance is outside, at the back of the building. It is reported to be on an accessible route from the parking lot.
• Restrooms inside the Visitor Center are reported to be on an accessible travel route. They do not meet UFAS. There is no stall at least 36 inches wide in either the men's or the women's restroom. No stall has a five-foot clear space. Sinks are accessible. In the men's room only, no stall door swings outward, and no stall has grab bars.
• There are two accessible water fountains.
• Public telephones are accessible. They may not have volume control and may not be compatible for use with hearing aids.

Campground

Devils Garden Campground

• There is one campsite designated for visitors with disabilities. Restrooms and water are reported to be accessible but details were not furnished. Cooking grills may not be accessible.

• The restroom in the group camping area is reported to be accessible.

Supplementary Information

• **Griffith River Expeditions** (P.O. Box 1324, 2231 S. Hwy. 191, Moab, UT 84532) offers whitewater raft trips, scenic float trips and a variety of seminar/specialty trips with guides and facilitators. Quoting from their questionnaire response: "Rivers offer access to country which may otherwise never be seen by people with disabilities. All our trips are offered to the disabled with special accommodations easily arranged. Serious medical needs may need to consider trips that remain close to town and emergency assistance."

Service has no restrictions. The staff has been sensitized and trained in regard to both adults and children having physical or mental disabilities. Experience with visitors who have developmental disabilities is stronger with children, who "do better" on trips closer to town. The concession has participated in programs with Horizons for the Handicapped Children's Hospital (Denver, Colorado).

Rafts are equipped with special frames to accommodate wheelchairs, crutches, etc. All guides have first-aid and CPR training; many are emergency medical technicians. Special coolers are carried for medications. Discounts are offered for companion caregivers. The current staff lacks sign language skills but has successfully served clients with hearing disabilities. Special reservations are recommended to assist in planning for any special services.

• **Tag-A-Long Tours** (452 N. Main St., Moab, UT 84532) offers a wide variety of interpretive tours, whitewater rafting and float trips. Interpretive tours by bus, van, four-wheel drive or boat go into the park and surrounding areas. This concession also serves Canyonlands N.P. See *Supplementary Information* section in that park for detailed description.

Basic Facilities

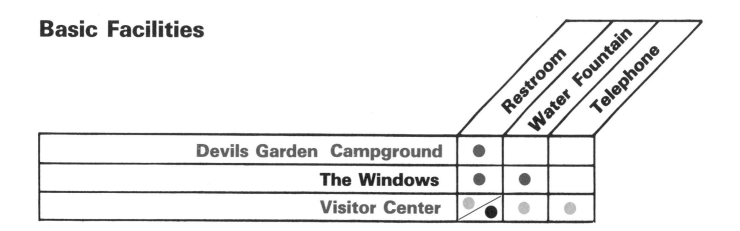

	Restroom	Water Fountain	Telephone
Devils Garden Campground	●		
The Windows	●	●	
Visitor Center	◐	○	○

Bryce Temple.

USGS—E.D. McKEE

Bryce Canyon

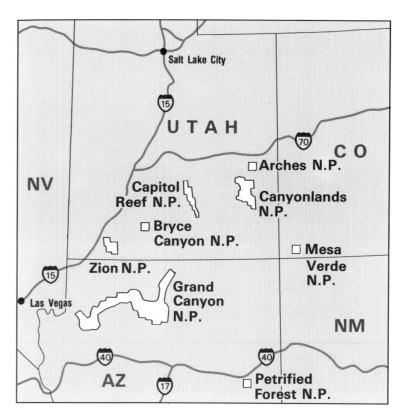

Superintendent
National Park Service
Bryce Canyon National Park
Bryce Canyon, UT 84717
Tel./TDD (801) 834-5322

Bryce Canyon is not a canyon at all but an amphitheater carved out of the Pink Cliffs. The natural beauty here truly defies written description and must be seen to be fully appreciated.

Walls and windows, minarets, gables, pagodas, pedestals and temples are all terms which have been used to describe the intricately-shaped landforms of Bryce Canyon. It is a common misconception that wind carved these formations. Water in the form of rain, snow and ice has been the primary erosional force responsible for creating the spectacular beauty and colorscapes of this geologic fantasyland.

The red limestone was deposited by vast lakes that once covered the area. Tectonic uplift has caused the plateau to be tilted higher on the southern end, producing a staircase effect. Descending the staircase south of the park to Zion and Grand Canyon, the rocks become progressively older. On the scale of geologic time, erosion in these badlands areas has been rapid. A thick soil layer has never been allowed to form and steep slopes prevent plants from taking root.

Nonetheless all is not barren rock at Bryce Canyon. There are forests here as well. The lower elevations support a dwarf forest of Utah juniper and piñon pine. On the plateau, ponderosa pine are most common and at the higher elevations spruce, aspen and fir take over. Spring and summer also offer beautiful wildflower displays including sego lily, penstemon, aster, evening primrose, Indian paintbrush and wild iris.

One enveloping factor provides the finishing touch to the grandeur of Bryce Canyon—Color. Throughout the day, from sunrise to sunset, light and shadow play upon the rocks spreading dazzling highlights of red, yellow, orange, purple and lavender. The red and yellow colors are caused by oxides of iron in the rocks; lavender and purple are caused by manganese.

General Information
Weather

The months of April through October are filled with pleasant days and cool nights. Conditions are generally dry, but thunderstorms are common during the summer. August is the wettest month. Snows can come as early as October and last until March or April. Many winter days are bright and crisp.

Climate Chart

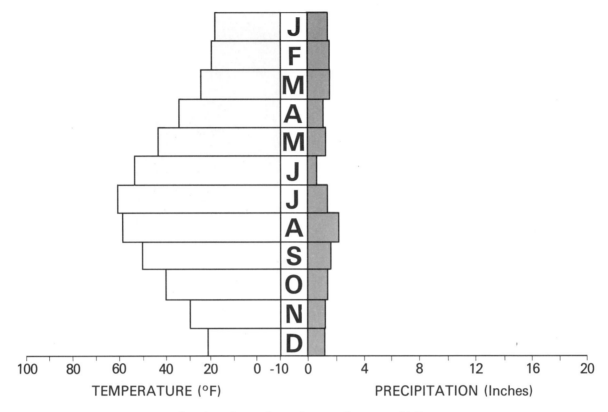

TEMPERATURE (°F)   PRECIPITATION (Inches)

Station Location: Bryce Canyon N.P.
Station Elevation: 7915 feet

Winter Visitation

The park is open all year, though some facilities are closed during winter. Some parts of the park receive up to ten feet of snow annually. Visitors may not be able to reach viewpoints or buildings until snow has been plowed. Temperatures can be cold.

Elevation

The average elevation of the main park features is 8000 to 9100 feet. The thin air can be dangerous for visitors with respiratory ailments or heart disease. Sunburn and overexertion should be guarded against.

Medical and Support Services

The nearest hospital is located in Panguitch, Utah, 26 miles from the park. The nearest complete range of services can be found in St. George, west of the park.

Publications

• A brochure entitled "Bryce Canyon National Park—Handicapped Access" is available from the Visitor Center or by writing to the park.
• The park newspaper, "Bryce Canyon Hoodoo," is produced seasonally and contains a wealth of general park information including segments about accessibility.
• Brochures are available that will inform visitors with disabilities of the physical requirements and other aspects of specific park resources.

Transportation

Private cars may be used for travel in the park. The park road is completely accessible to private cars, except immediately following snowstorms. A van is run from the Lodge but it is not accessible. No other means of transportation are available.

Medical and Support Services

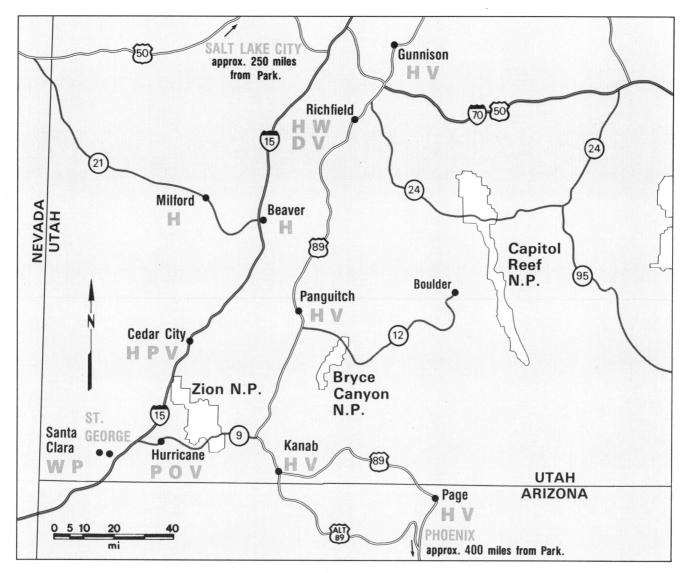

Sign Language Interpreter

There are no park personnel with signing skills currently on staff. Occasionally a seasonal employee is hired who has had training in ASL, so visitors should inquire. Arrangements exist for contacting an interpreter through the park radio system in the event of an emergency.

TDD

There is TDD capability in the park. The number is (801) 834-5322.

Dog Guides

Dog guides are permitted in the park.

Programs

Organized Programs

Naturalist-led activities are subject to budgetary changes so visitors should check at the Visitor Center for current listings. Some activities are conducted in accessible locations but they may vary from year to year.

Park personnel use descriptive, concrete language during program narratives.

Not all programs utilize items that can be touched. Park personnel use simple verbal presentations and basic reasoning techniques with as much "hands on" participation as possible.

• A seven-minute orientation slide program is shown at the **Visitor Center**. The auditorium is accessible.

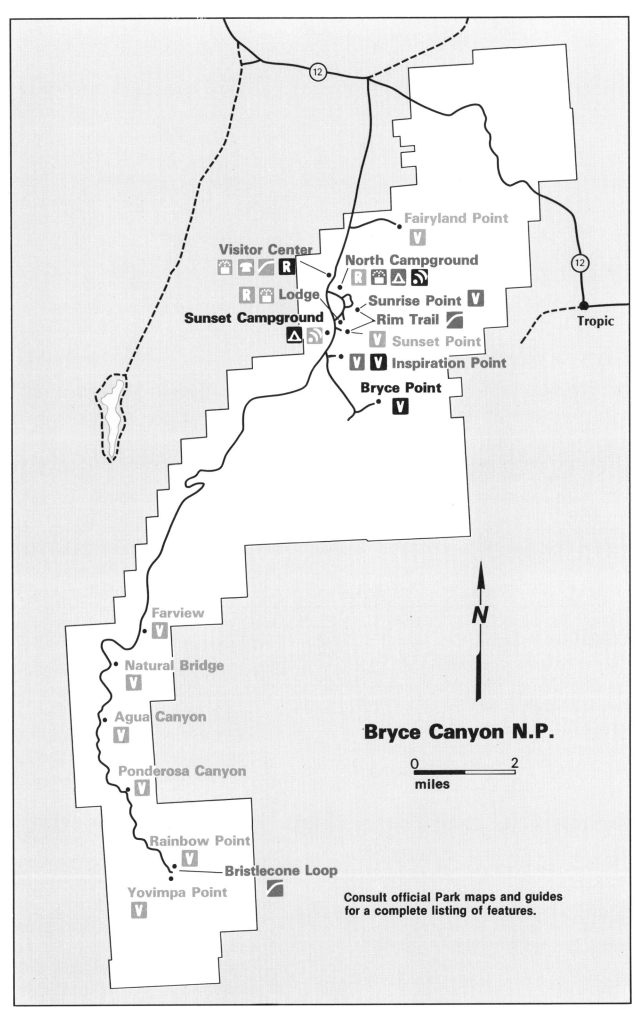

Fairyland Point

Visitor Center

North Campground

Lodge

Sunrise Point

Rim Trail

Sunset Campground

Sunset Point

Inspiration Point

Bryce Point

Tropic

N

Bryce Canyon N.P.

0   2

miles

Farview

Natural Bridge

Agua Canyon

Ponderosa Canyon

Consult official Park maps and guides for a complete listing of features.

Rainbow Point

Bristlecone Loop

Yovimpa Point

Park roads range from 8000 to just over 9000 ft. in elevation.

• Evening programs, including slide shows, are given by a naturalist during the summer at **Sunset Campground Amphitheater**, which is accessible. Allowances have been made for wheelchair users in the program seating area. There are accessible restrooms and water, and an accessible path from parking to the restrooms and the amphitheater.

• A 20-minute geology talk is held at **Sunset Point**. The program area is accessible. The parking area, restrooms and water are also accessible.

• The Rim Walk begins at **Bryce Lodge** and lasts about one hour. The Lodge has accessible restrooms and water, but the parking area is not accessible. The **Rim Trail** is reported to be accessible (see *Trails* section).

• A quarter-mile naturalist-led walk to a prairie dog town originates at the **Visitor Center** and is accessible to wheelchair users. This summer program lasts about an hour. Visitors should check for current schedule.

Self-Guided Programs

• A trail guide is available for the Queen's Garden Trail. This self-guided program was not evaluated for accessibility.

• All park viewpoints and most buildings are accessible from parking lots. Most viewpoints are easily accessible to visitors in wheelchairs. Visitors may find it beneficial to have assistance to and from some overlooks.

• **Fairyland Point, Sunrise Point, Sunset Point, Inspiration Point** and **Bryce Point** have parking for visitors with disabilities. Some viewpoints have accessible restrooms. Visitors using wheelchairs may have to view some scenic vistas through wire security fences.

Trails

• The **Rim Trail** between **Sunrise Point** and **Sunset Point** is suitable for wheelchairs. This one-half mile section of trail is relatively flat and is paved. The trail offers exceptional views of the Queens Garden formation. Assistance for wheelchair users may be required in places along the trail.

• The **Bristlecone Loop** is a one-mile gravel trail beginning at **Rainbow Point**. Short sections of the trail near Rainbow Point may be appropriate for wheelchair users. The trail has some steep hills which would be difficult or dangerous for a wheelchair user to negotiate, even with assistance. This trail stays on top of the plateau and meanders through stretches of Douglas fir and white fir before ending in a forest of bristlecone pine.

Exhibits

• A seven-minute automatic slide program, providing well-illustrated information about the park environment, is shown at the **Visitor Center**. Slide presentations have been transcribed into print.

• The upper shelves of book sale exhibits are not accessible.

• Most exhibits are not accessible to wheelchair users but construction of new exhibits is imminent.

• Exhibit lighting is often inadequate. Interpretive labels have not been designed for maximum contrast. Some interpretive signs have been routed but many are made of smooth fiberglass.

• Some exhibits utilize photographs, pictorial illustrations and other means to help visitors appreciate the park.

• Currently there are no tactile exhibits in the park but a "touch room" is planned for the **Visitor Center** museum.

Visitor Center

• There is reserved, signed parking approximately 180 feet from the Visitor Center. The reserved spaces are not extrawide. Necessary curb cuts are in place. The parking area is paved blacktop and is level and smooth.

• The parking area is lower than the visitor center. There is a continuous route of travel from the parking area to the main entrance which is reported to be usable. Assistance is likely necessary. The pathway is composed of sandstone slabs. There may be level changes greater than one-half inch which have not been beveled. A ramp is in use on this route. Its rise is greater than 1:12, so assistance is needed. The ramp is four feet, ten inches wide, equipped with handrails and edging, but the surface is sandstone and may be slippery when wet. (The ramp may become icy in winter. Ice is routinely removed.)

• One section of the information desk and a section of the sales counter are accessible to wheelchair users.

• Restrooms are not accessible but may be usable. There is no stall in either the men's or women's restroom which is at least 36 inches wide, but the stall doors do swing outward. These stalls do not have a five-foot clear space to allow for turning a wheelchair. Toilets, urinals, sinks, grab bars and other features have been properly positioned for wheelchair users but sinks do not have adequate clearance underneath. Faucet levers have protruding ends and are easy to turn. Soap dispensers and mirrors have been lowered.

• The water fountain is reported to be accessible for wheelchair users.

• There is an accessible telephone at the Visitor Center. It does not have a volume control, but it is hearing-aid compatible.

• There is TDD capability available. The number is (801) 834-5322.

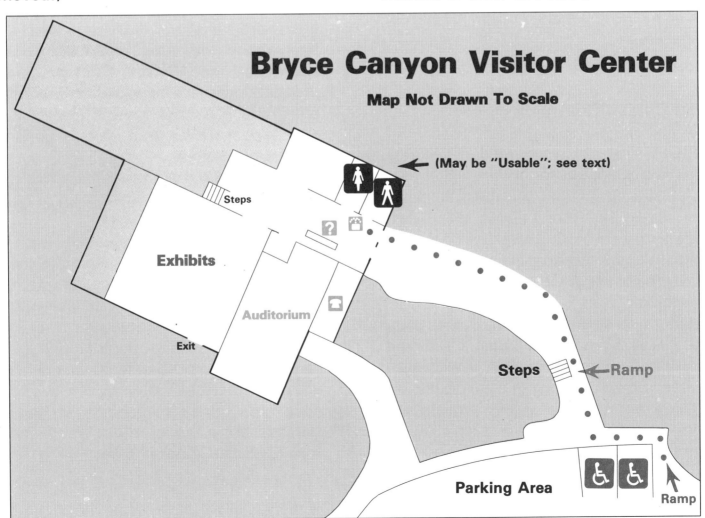

Bryce Canyon Visitor Center

Map Not Drawn To Scale

← (May be "Usable"; see text)

Steps

Exhibits

Auditorium

Exit

Steps ← Ramp

Parking Area

Ramp

Campgrounds

North Campground

• There are two designated campsites. They are reserved for visitors with disabilities until 6:00 p.m. each day. ***Note:*** *No reserved sites are available in winter.*

• Loop D, Site 95— The parking area is about three feet from the campsite. The surface is fine crushed stone and is uneven. There is a level black-top route to the campsite.

• Loop D, Site 97— The parking space is not extra-wide and is approximately 16 feet from the campsite. The parking area surface is uneven, finely crushed stone. The route of travel from the parking area to the campsite is over uneven, finely-crushed stone.

• Restroom facilities are accessible. There is inadequate clear space in the stalls to allow turning of a wheelchair. The sinks have been fitted with wrist control faucets. Mirrors have been adjusted to proper heights.

• The water source is reported to be accessible. It is a faucet with hand levers.

• Cooking grills are reported to be fully accessible. At the picnic table, clearance from the ground to the table bottom is 29.5 inches.

Sunset Campground does not have any campsites that are specifically designed or especially appropriate for visitors with disabilities.

Agua Canyon displays intricate beauty in stone.

USGS — E.D. McKEE

Supplementary Information

• **Bryce Canyon Lodge** (P.O. Box 400, 451 N. Main St., Cedar City, UT 84720) A published source reports that "some lodging" and "all other facilities are accessible." No other details were furnished by the concession.

• **Bryce Zion Trail Rides** (P.O. Box 58, Tropic, UT 84776) offers guided horseback trips into the park. Service is not restricted. Participants must have good balance, be able to hold onto the saddle and have no fear of heights. Staff has had no specialized sensitivity training in serving clients with disabilities. However, publishers are in receipt of an extremely laudatory letter from a participant who witnessed the excellent service rendered to an individual with speech and motor disabilities. Staff has had no experience providing service to wheelchair users or clients with profound visual disabilities.

Staff has worked successfully with clients with hearing disabilities, developmental disabilities and special medical needs. Staff expresses an enthusiastic willingness to work with visitors with disabilities and will do what is necessary to assist.

• **Bryce Canyon Natural History Association** operates a retail store in the park. Books, maps, calendars, postcards and other interpretive information is for sale. Staff has experience serving patrons with a wide range of disabilities. Staff has been sensitized to the needs of visitors with disabilities but has received no extensive training. Staff is willing to assist. The concession is located in the Visitor Center; see above for parking/access. The store interior is accessible. It features an open sales area (no aisles). Bookcases are seven feet high; the top shelf is 64 inches from the floor. Vending machines have operating controls lower than 54 inches.

Basic Facilities

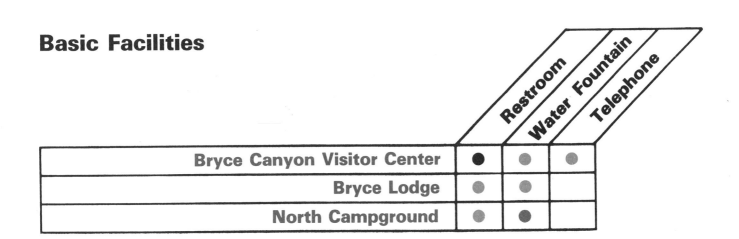

	Restroom	Water Fountain	Telephone
Bryce Canyon Visitor Center	●	●	●
Bryce Lodge	●	●	
North Campground	●	●	

Canyonlands

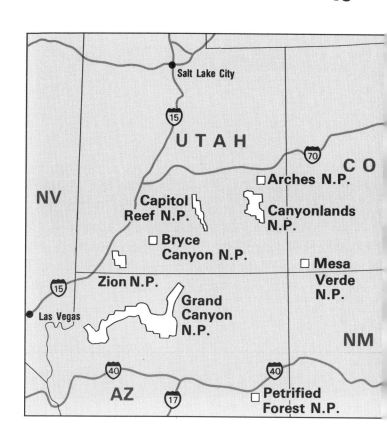

Superintendent
Canyonlands National Park
Moab, UT 84532
Tel. (801) 259-7164

Canyonlands National Park is situated in the heart of the Colorado Plateau. Water and wind have chiseled this landscape, carving out hundreds of canyons, mesas and buttes. The two largest canyons have been cut by the Green and Colorado Rivers. These two major watercourses divide the park into three distinct regions: Island in the Sky to the north, the Maze to the west, and the Needles to the east. Each of these areas offers its own special taste of the desert environment.

Views from the scenic overlooks in Island in the Sky stretch nearly 100 miles to the horizon. Vegetation in the Island consists of a variety of grass species and pygmy piñon-juniper forests. Coyotes, foxes, ravens and hawks all search this area for food. The largest population of bighorn sheep in the park also inhabits this section.

The Maze is one of the most remote and inaccessible places in the entire United States. This area of the park registers the least number of visitors due to its remoteness and seemingly endless confusion of canyons, towers, mesas and buttes.

The Needles section has been aptly named for its rock spires and pinnacles. This area is host to a large collection of strange and beautiful geologic formations.

Visitors to Canyonlands will be able to view pre-historic pictographs painted on the walls of Horseshoe Canyon or see the stone and mud dwellings at Tower Ruins left by the Anasazi. These Native Americans were part of the same group of people that built the pueblos at Mesa Verde in Colorado. Visitors who choose only to drive the park roads are treated to some of the finest wild canyonland scenery anywhere in the world.

General Information
Weather

The park's desert climate is characterized by hot summers, pleasant spring and fall months and cool winters. Low humidity partially offsets the heat of summer. Precipitation is sparse with most falling in the form of late summer and early autumn thunderstorms. Winter snowfall is usually light.

Daily summer temperatures range from 80 to 100°F in the day and in the 50's at

Climate Chart

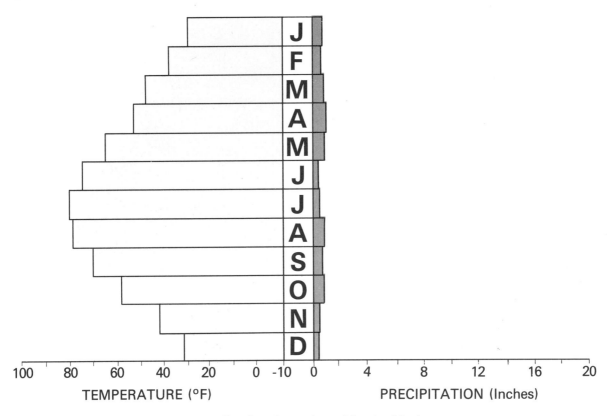

TEMPERATURE (°F)   PRECIPITATION (Inches)

Station Location: Moab, Utah
Station Elevation: 3965 feet

night. Spring and fall daytime highs commonly range from 60 to 80° and nights from 20 to 50°. Winter daytime temperatures range from 30 to 50° with nightly lows from 0 to 20°.

Safety

Visitors should be prepared for the heat and should rest occasionally to avoid over-exertion. Walk carefully on "slick-rock" surfaces; it is also easy to get stranded or to slip on sandy surfaces. Most animals, including poisonous snakes and scorpions, rarely cause injuries unless disturbed. Flash floods can occur without warning. Never camp in a dry wash or drive across a flooded area. Avoid over-exposure to cold and wet conditions, especially on the rivers, which can lead to hypothermia. There is no drinking water in the park, except seasonally in Squaw Flat Campground in the Needles District.

Winter Visitation

The park is open during winter. Special considerations include cold temperatures, snow and slick roads.

Elevation

Elevations in the park range from 5000 feet in the Needles District to 6300 feet in the Island District. Visitors with heart or respiratory problems should guard against overexertion.

Medical and Support Services

The nearest hospitals are located in Moab and Monticello, Utah. A complete range of services can be found in Salt Lake City, Utah and Grand Junction, Colorado.

Publications

There are no publications available that directly address the needs of visitors with disabilities. Brochure information about the physical requirements and other aspects of specific park resources is available but limited.

Medical and Support Services

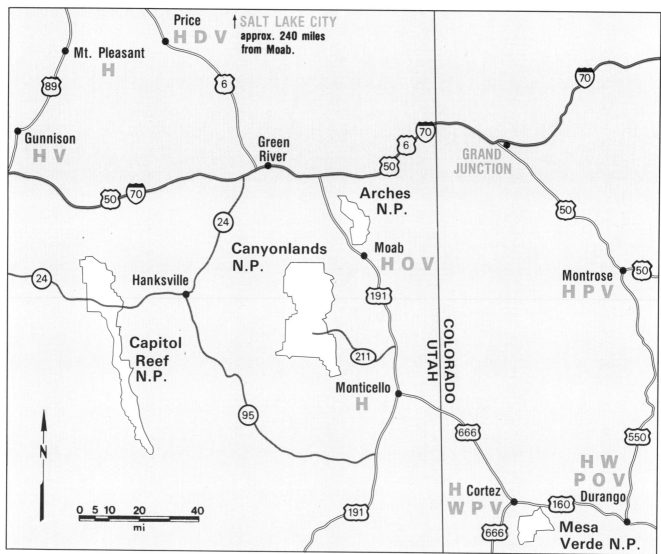

Transportation

Private cars may be used for travel in the park. There are paved roads into Needles and Island in the Sky Districts. The roads into the Maze District are graded dirt.

Sign Language Interpreter

Currently there are no park personnel with signing skills on staff. There are no pre-arrangements to contact an interpreter in the event of an emergency. Seasonal personnel may be hired that have signing skills but they may not be present every year. Special interpretive programs may be scheduled well in advance, but only if a qualified guide is available.

TDD

There is no TDD capability within the park.

Sighted Guide Method

Park personnel are only moderately familiar with the Sighted Guide Method. Inquire in advance for current status.

Dog Guides

Dog guides are permitted in the park but special arrangements must be made for back-country use.

Programs
Organized Programs

Most programs are conducted in areas not convenient for visitors with mobility impairments.

Programs using sign language interpreters may be scheduled if a skilled person is hired for the summer but such personnel may not be present from year to year.

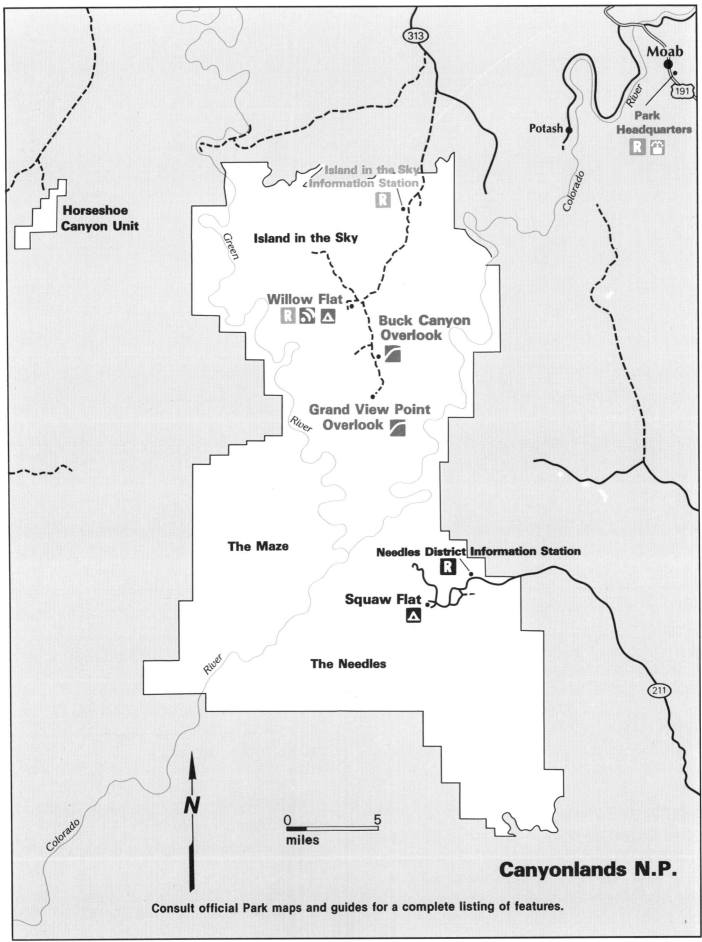

Moab

313

191

Potash

Park
Headquarters

Island in the Sky
Information Station

Island in the Sky

Green

Colorado

Horseshoe
Canyon Unit

Willow Flat

Buck Canyon
Overlook

Grand View Point
Overlook

River

The Maze

Needles District Information Station

Squaw Flat

River

The Needles

211

N

Colorado

0   5
miles

Canyonlands N.P.

Consult official Park maps and guides for a complete listing of features.

Park roads range from 5000 to 6400 ft. in elevation.

Park personnel use descriptive, concrete language, photographs, pictorial illustrations and other means as necessary during program narratives.

During programs park personnel may include items that can be touched.

• Interpretive programs are given at an amphitheater in the **Willow Flat Campground**. The area is level but not paved. It is reported to be wheelchair accessible. Accessible vault toilets are located in the campground.

• The program areas in the **Squaw Flat Campground** are not wheelchair accessible. Usually they are located on a large rock; in inclement weather a small cave is used. Visitors with other mobility impairments should contact a Ranger to determine access potential.

Self-Guided Programs

Most self-guided programs are in locations that are not accessible to wheelchair users. The best area to try is the Island in the Sky area, where all major roads are paved and installation of new wayside exhibits is imminent. These exhibits will be 31 inches high with a 31° angle of display.

Trails

None of the park's trails have been designed for visitors with mobility impairments. However, a 100-foot section of the **Buck Canyon** Overlook Trail and a 100-foot section of the **Grand View** Point Trail are paved. These two sections of trail are at least 36 inches wide with an asphalt surface. The Grand View section does not exceed a 1:20 grade while the Buck Canyon section does not exceed 1:16. There are no sheltered rest areas, restrooms or water along these trail sections. There are no barriers to obstruct the view for visitors in wheelchairs.

Exhibits

• General information exhibits about the park environment that are well-illustrated by photographs or other pictorial means may be found at **Island in the Sky Infor-**mation Station. The horizontal exhibits here have bottom surfaces with a minimum clearance of 27 inches from ground level to allow a frontal approach by wheelchair users. These exhibits have adjacent clear space to allow approach by wheelchair users.

• Adequate and even lighting is used to display exhibits. High-contrast photographs and non-glare glass have both been incorporated into exhibit design.

• Interpretive labels have been designed for maximum contrast.

• Special tactile exhibit objects for visitors with visual impairments are available at the Visitor Information Stations at **Needles** and **Island in the Sky**.

• Not all tactile exhibits are placed on work surfaces 28 to 34 inches from ground level or within 24-inch reach.

• Interpretive signs are fiberglass impregnated and metal and are not routed or raised.

Visitor Centers

Park Headquarters Visitor Center

• Located in Moab, Utah. This Visitor Center provides information for both Canyonlands and Arches National Parks.

• There is reserved, signed parking about 50 feet from the Visitor Center. Spaces are not extra-wide. The parking area is level and smooth asphalt. Accessible curb cuts are in place.

• There is a continuous accessible route from the reserved parking to the main entrance. The route is at least three feet wide and is level, smooth cement. The main entrance has two sets of hinged glass doors which are difficult for wheelchair users to open. Assistance may be necessary.

• The information desk is higher than 34 inches.

• The restrooms are reported to be fully accessible. However, the men's restroom lacks a urinal placed properly for wheelchair users.

• There is an accessible water fountain.

• There is no public telephone at this Visitor Center. However, if needed, a telephone is available for calls during working hours.

Island In The Sky Visitor Center

This Visitor Center is a new modular frame building. It is reported to be totally accessible, including the information desk and exhibits. All walkways are smooth. Accessible vault toilets are in place.

Needles District Contact Station

The Needles District Contact Station is a small trailer house that is not accessible for wheelchair users. The entrance has two steps and the door is narrow. The parking area is paved. The restrooms at the contact station are inaccessible pit toilets.

Campgrounds

Willow Flat Campground

• Parking at Willow Flat does not meet UFAS. It is reported to be very sandy but usable for some wheelchair users. Assistance may be required.

• Accessible vault toilets are in place.

• There is no water source at Willow Flat.

• Cooking grills are reported to be accessible. There are four accessible picnic tables at the Campground.

Squaw Flat Campground does not have any campsites that are specifically designed or especially appropriate for visitors with disabilities. Restroom facilities are not accessible for wheelchair users.

Supplementary Information

• **Adrift Adventures** (P.O. Box 81032, Salt Lake City, UT 84108 or 378 No. Main Street, Moab, UT 84532) offers float trips, river rafting, park sightseeing (by van and jeep) and other services. Half-day, full-day and multiple-day trips are possible. Staff has had limited sensitization training

in serving the needs of clients with disabilities but its experience has been wide including: wheelchair users, clients with visual and hearing disabilities, and those with special medical needs. Experience has included special programs sponsored by the National Football League and the United Way. The United Way programs have included children with developmental or other disabilities. Individual participants and concession staff review needs and select an appropriate trip. Wheelchairs can be accommodated on the rafts. "Walk-ins" can arrange for daily trips; all multiple-day trips require reservations from any group or individual.

• **Don Hatch River Expeditions** (P.O. Box 1150, 221 N. 400 East, Vernal, UT 84078 offers whitewater rafting. Quoting from questionnaire response: "We are capable of taking a wide range of people with disabilities. In the past we have taken people with blindness, deafness and mentally retarded. They should be capable of getting in and out of a boat, holding on through rapids, capable of living outdoors . . . Disabled should be able to move on rough terrain, get in and out of boat(s), capable of packing some light items, taking direction for water/rapids survival." Staff is experienced in guiding visitors with disabilities and has advanced first-aid training. Past experience includes serving a youth group with developmental disabilities. Clients with special medical needs, such as diabetics, have been served successfully. The concession has had no experience serving clients using wheelchairs. Reservations, as required for any group, are needed.

• **Griffith River Expeditions** (P.O. Box 1324, 2231 S. Hwy. 191, Moab, UT 84532) offers whitewater raft trips, scenic float trips and a variety of seminar/specialty trips with guides and facilitators. This concession also serves Arches N.P. See *Supplementary Information* under that park for details.

Angel Arch in the Needles.

• **Moki Mac River Expeditions** (P.O. Box 21242, Salt Lake City, UT 84121) offers a wide variety of motorized river trips and whitewater rafting. Many trips are rugged and remote in nature and clients must consider their personal capabilities. Staff has had no formal sensitization training regarding clients with disabilities but has had successful experiences in this area. Concession has had no experience with clients with profound visual disabilities but has served those with mobility impairments (including wheelchair users) and hearing impairments. Experience with clients with special medical needs has been limited to those with dietary restrictions, such as clients with diabetes. Staff is willing to assist clients with disabilities.

• **Tag-A-Long Tours** (452 N. Main St., Moab, UT 84532) offers a wide variety of interpretive tours, whitewater rafting and float trips. Interpretive tours by bus, van, four-wheel-drive or boat go into the park and surrounding areas. Stops may include visitor centers, scenic overlooks and other points of interest. All trips originate and terminate at the Moab headquarters where there is signed, reserved parking on a smooth, level surface. Access to the bus involves three 1-foot steps (handrail present, ramp available). Access

to the van involves one 2-foot step. Access to the boat involves one 1-foot step and seating. In all cases the concession operator will give assistance where required. Vehicles have no other adaptations. Special arrangements can be made for transporting clients with disabilities; depending on circumstances, there may be an additional charge.

Whitewater/flat water boat trips and four-wheel-drive expeditions range from one-half day to six days. Quoting from their questionnaire response: "We don't feel that any person will have trouble, provided that they are very comfortable with water and are able to walk about a half-block in sand. (We will carry those who can't.) There is some jarring and bouncing on these trips."

Staff has been sensitized to the needs of clients with disabilities and has experience in serving a wide range of clients with disabilities, including wheelchair users, hearing impaired or deaf, visually impaired or blind, and those with special medical needs. (Overnight trips are one day's travel from medical facilities.) Staff is also experienced serving clients with developmental disabilities when accompanied by a caregiver: "Everything was fine, again provided they are comfortable with water." Groups must make reservations at least one week ahead.

Basic Facilities

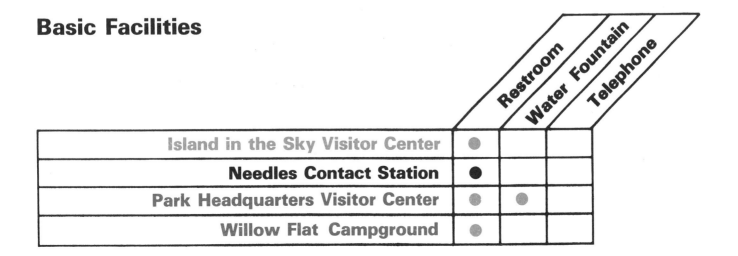

	Restroom	Water Fountain	Telephone
Island in the Sky Visitor Center	●		
Needles Contact Station	●		
Park Headquarters Visitor Center	●	●	
Willow Flat Campground	●		

Capitol Reef

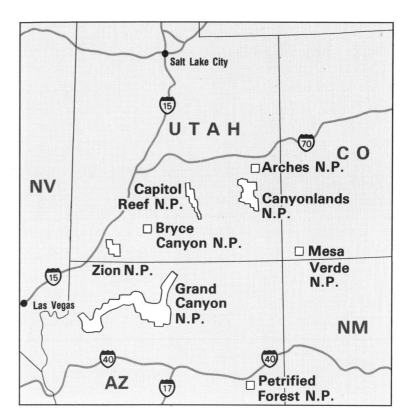

Accessibility Coordinator
National Park Service
Capitol Reef National Park
Torrey, UT 84775
Tel. (801) 425-3791

Capitol Reef is located in southern Utah on the Colorado Plateau. The "reef" familiar to present-day visitors is the prominent, eroded cliff extending south from the Visitor Center. It was described as a "reef" by early travelers through the area because it represented a barrier to passage. The "capitol" portion of the park's name is derived from a white sandstone dome that resembles the dome of the U.S. Capitol. Much of the park is a rugged wilderness composed of canyons, gorges, arches and steep cliff faces. The visitor to Capitol Reef will first be met by the contrasting landscapes of the lush Fremont River valley and the drier, barren cliffs and terraces of the reef.

Life has adapted itself to this harsh, dry climate. On some of the gentler slopes will be found piñon pine and Utah juniper. Most of the larger land animals such as the ringtail cat, fox, coyote, deer and mountain lion prefer to come out at night and during the early morning hours. This is a land of extreme conditions for any species to survive in.

While most of Capitol Reef's quarter-million acres are remote back country, there is still much to be seen. There are several routes through the park that are accessible by passenger car. Utah Route 24 has many scenic pullouts. The Scenic Drive, a well-maintained gravel road, leads to Grand Wash and Capitol Gorge. Dirt roads are more suited to vehicles with higher ground clearance. Visitors should check with the rangers at the Visitor Center for recommendations.

General Information
Weather

The high elevations and desert climate of Capitol Reef make the area prone to temperature extremes. Daytime highs in June and July are commonly in the upper 90's °F while nights may dip into the 50's. Heavy thunderstorms can cause flash floods from July through September.

Spring and fall are mild with warm days and cool nights. Daytime temperatures in winter usually hover between 40 and 50° but may drop below freezing at night. Bitter cold temperatures can occur but are not common. Snowfall is light. Humidity is low and precipitation is sparse, totaling less than seven inches per year.

Winter Visitation

The park is open during winter. Visitors should check at the Visitor Center for

Climate Chart

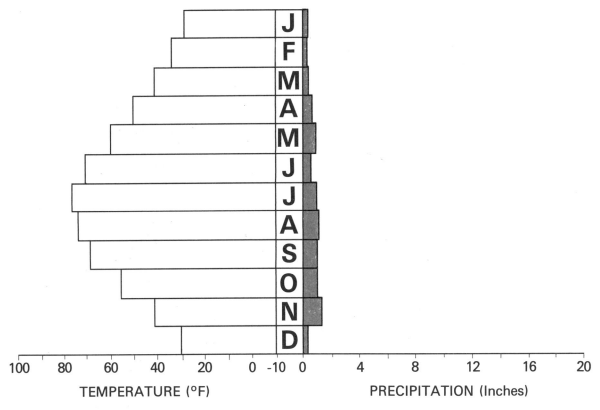

TEMPERATURE (°F)   PRECIPITATION (Inches)

Station Location: Capitol Reef N.P.
Station Elevation: 5500 feet

road and weather conditions. One section of the Main Campground remains open but the dumping station and water are shut off.

Safety
Beware of possible flash floods.

Elevation
Elevation of park roads ranges from 5200 to 7000 feet. Visitors coming via Utah Route 12 from Bryce Canyon will travel over a 9400-foot summit. The average elevation from which main park features can be viewed is 5400 feet. High altitudes can cause problems for visitors with heart or respiratory conditions. Visitors should caution against overexertion.

Medical and Support Services
The nearest hospitals are located in Richfield, Gunnison and Panguitch, Utah. A complete range of services can be found in St. George, southwest of the park and in Salt Lake City, 220 miles north of the park.

Publications
• There are no publications available that directly address the needs of visitors with disabilities.
• Brochures about the physical requirements and other aspects of specific park resources are available at the Visitor Center.
• A cassette tape and player and a printed script are available for the self-guiding Scenic Drive Auto Tour.

Transportation
Private cars may be used for travel in the park. Check at the Visitor Center for current road conditions. Roads into the North (Cathedral Valley) and South Districts are unimproved. High-clearance or four-wheel drive vehicles are recommended for travel in the North District.

Sign Language Interpreter
There are no park personnel with signing skills currently on staff. There are no

Medical and Support Services

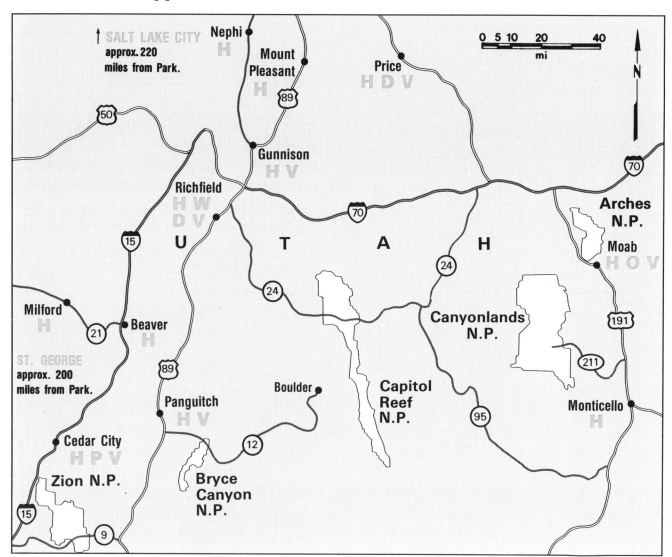

pre-arrangements to contact an inter-preter in the event of an emergency.

TDD

There is no TDD capability within the park.

Dog Guides

Dog guides are permitted in the park.

Programs

Organized Programs

• Program locations and content may vary from year to year. Programs listed in this section are representative of a typical season.

• Park personnel at the **Visitor Center** can provide information on the availability and location of alternative interpretive devices and services for visitors with visual or hearing impairments.

• Not all organized programs are conducted in physically accessible locations. Evening programs are held at the **Amphitheater** which is reached via packed earth/gravel paths leading from the lower ends of **Main Campground** Loops B and C and from the Amphitheater parking area. Accessible restrooms and water are located 250 feet from the Amphitheater at the end of the path to Campground Loop C. There are no designated areas for wheelchairs in the Amphitheater but there is ample room along the aisles.

• A history walk is conducted along a portion of Scenic Drive (one mile south of the **Visitor Center**) and passes an accessible restroom facility at the picnic area near the end of the trip.

• A ten-minute introductory slide presentation is offered at the **Visitor Center**.

Wheelchair users can use the left entrance to the theater. It is 33 inches wide. The theater can accommodate two wheelchairs per showing.

• Park personnel use descriptive, concrete language during program narratives. This is particularly true if visitors with visual impairments are present. In a limited number of programs, park personnel utilize objects that may be touched. Involvement of other senses is stressed as well.

• Photographs, pictorial illustrations and other means of clear communication are used during the wildlife workshop.

• Park personnel use simple verbal presentations and basic reasoning techniques to communicate with visitors with developmental disabilities. There are no scheduled programs specially designed for visitors with developmental disabilities. Contact the interpretive staff to arrange special group tours. Arrangements for visitors with developmental disabilities are rarely possible due to small staff size.

• A-V programs are held in the **Visitor Center** and the **Amphitheater**. Both facilities are accessible although some persons may require assistance negotiating ramps or graveled paths.

Self-Guided Programs

• The park has six published self-guiding tour pamphlets available for visitors. The Hickman Bridge and Chimney Rock Canyon self-guiding trails are not accessible for wheelchair users. Accessibility of others is described below.

• The initial one-half to three-quarter-mile section of the Fremont River Trail is reported to be accessible to wheelchair users. (See also *Trails*.) A booklet is available at the trailhead located adjacent to the **Amphitheater** parking area.

• The Scenic Drive Auto Tour guide booklet (25-mile round trip) is available at the **Visitor Center**. This tour is available in audio form and may be obtained from the Visitor Center. The taped program uses highly descriptive language and provides virtually all the relevant park resource information that would be acquired through sight. Roadside turnouts are found along the tour route. There is a **Picnic Area** three-quarters of a mile south of the Visitor Center (one-quarter mile north of the Campground). It has accessible restrooms.

• A newspaper guide for the Cathedral Valley Auto Tour is also available at the **Visitor Center**. High-clearance or four-wheel drive vehicles are recommended for this arduous 60-mile tour. Most of the scenic views can be enjoyed from a vehicle.

• The Historic Fruita Sojurn is a walking or driving tour. A self-guiding pamphlet is available. The tour is reported to be accessible except for the first stop where a steep path leads to an overlook of the Fruita historic area.

Trails

• The Fremont River Trail is the only accessible trail for wheelchair users in the park. There is an accessible path of travel from the **Amphitheater** parking area to the trailhead. The first three-quarters of a mile of the trail is quite level and firmly packed and has proven "usable" by visitors in wheelchairs. The trail has a contrasting walkway surface that stands out from the surrounding terrain. Printed information about the trail is available at the trailhead located adjacent to the Amphitheater parking area.

Exhibits

• Well-illustrated general information about the park is available at the **Visitor Center**.

• Some vertical signs and exhibits are coincidentally accessible to visitors with mobility impairments. A number of exhibit signs are located above the maximum reading height of 65 inches. Lettering is generally large and in bold-face type but could present problems to seated visitors wearing bifocals.

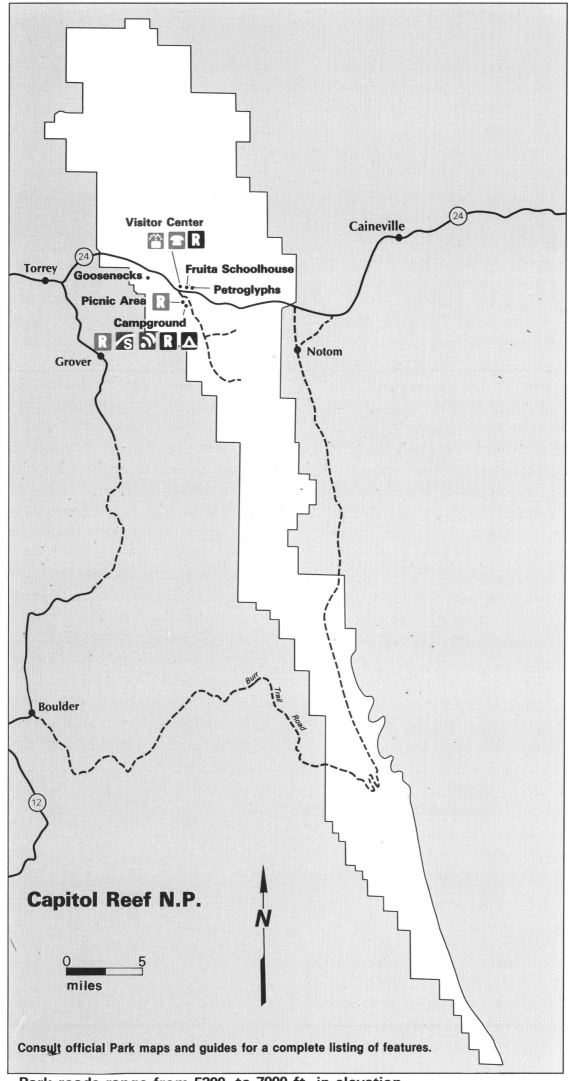

Capitol Reef N.P.

N

0   5
miles

Park roads range from 5200 to 7000 ft. in elevation.

Consult official Park maps and guides for a complete listing of features.

• Exhibits are located at the **Visitor Center**, Capitol Gorge and at several historic structures and points of interest along Utah Route 24 and the Scenic Drive. Taped audio messages are found at the Fruita Schoolhouse and the Blacksmith Shop. All horizontal wayside exhibits have bottom surfaces a minimum of 27 inches from ground level to allow a frontal approach by a wheelchair user. The exhibits at the **Visitor Center** have adjacent clear space to allow approach by a wheelchair user. These exhibits also have horizontal top surfaces designed to be viewed from an average eye level height of 48 inches. Items to be manipulated are mounted at a maximum height of 54 inches allowing a side approach, and a maximum height of 48 inches allowing a frontal approach by wheelchair users.

• Most book racks are higher than 40 inches from ground level. Other exhibits may or may not be placed on a work surface 28 to 34 inches from ground level and within a 24-inch reach.

• Adequate, even lighting and high contrast colors on photographs have been used in exhibit design. Interpretive labels have been designed for maximum contrast.

• A tactile exhibit is located at the **Visitor Center** where an "open" display is available allowing fossils, dinosaur bones, dinosaur track casts and textures of various specimens to be touched.

• Wayside and **Visitor Center** exhibits use simple photographs, pictorial illustrations and other means to assist visitors with developmental disabilities to appreciate park features.

Visitor Center

• There is reserved, signed, accessible parking in front of the Visitor Center. The reserved parking is about 50 feet from the building. The parking area is paved, level and smooth. One reserved parking space has a width of 18½ feet. This also serves as a loading zone. There is a curb cut and ramp adjacent to the loading zone. The ramp has a 1:9 slope, so assistance may be necessary. Edging is in place on the ramp.

• A smooth concrete sidewalk is inclined (1:7 slope) between the curb and the building entrance landings.

• The information desk is higher than 34 inches.

• The only accessible restrooms in the park are located in campground Loop C and in the picnic area, three-quarters of a mile south of the Visitor Center along the Scenic Drive.

• In the Visitor Center, the restroom doorways do not permit entry by a visitor using a wheelchair. Toilet facilities have not been modified for accessibility, although at least one stall door in each restroom swings outward. There is at least one sink in both the women's and men's restrooms positioned at an accessible height. Faucet fittings are easy to turn.

• The water fountain is inside the Visitor Center. The spout is no higher than 36 inches from the floor and allows for use of a cup. The lever moves easily.

• The public telephone is located at the building level. The position and features of the telephone are accessible to wheelchair users, however it does not have a volume control and is not hearing-aid compatible.

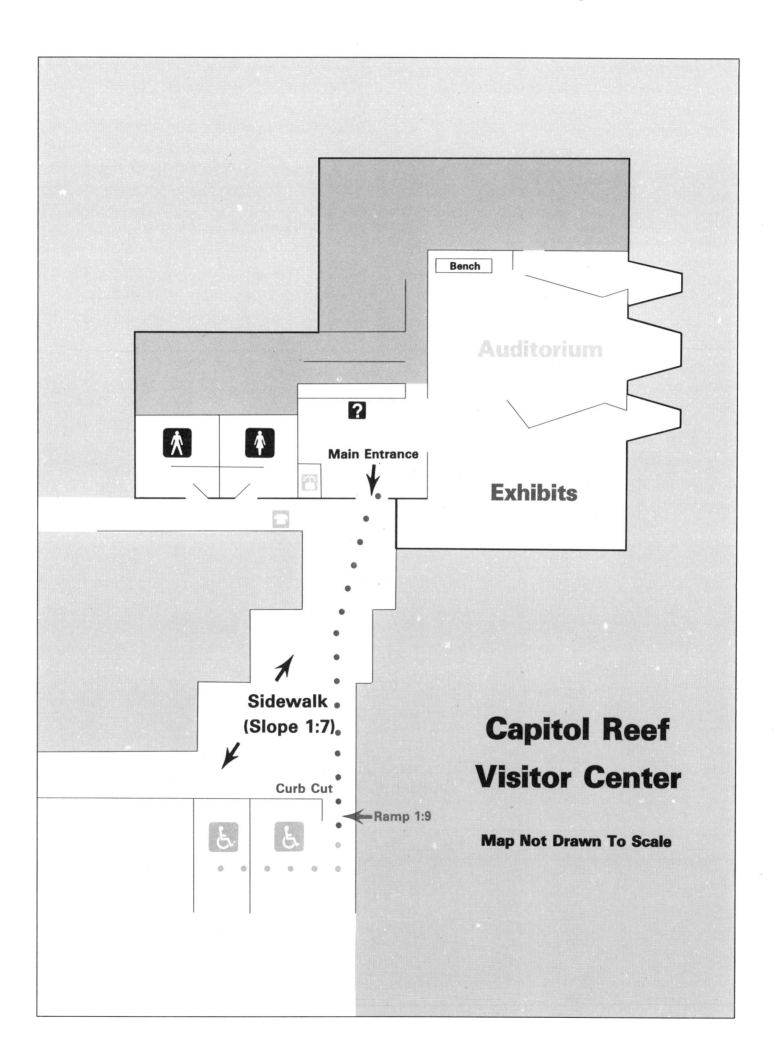

Bench

Auditorium

Main Entrance

Exhibits

Sidewalk
(Slope 1:7)

Curb Cut

Ramp 1:9

Capitol Reef

Visitor Center

Map Not Drawn To Scale

Campgrounds

Main Campground

• There are no designated campsites. No sites have features appropriate for visitors with disabilities.

• Only the restroom in Loop C is accessible. Another accessible restroom facility is located on the Scenic Drive, one-quarter mile north of the Main Campground.

• The water sources at the Main Campground are accessible. Faucets are operated by knobs.

• The cooking grills are reported to be accessible. The ground surface adjacent to some grills is not level.

• Reservations are required only for groups.

Cathedral Valley and **Cedar Mesa Campgrounds** offer a wilderness camping experience. They do not have any facilities that are specially designed for visitors with disabilities.

Supplementary Information

• **Capitol Reef Natural History Association** operates a retail store in the park. (It is located in the Visitor Center. See *Visitor Center* section for access information.) Staff has had experience serving patrons with a wide range of disabilities and has been sensitized to their needs. Staff is willing to give assistance as needed. Sales area is open (no aisles) and accessible. Maximum shelf height is 60.5 inches. The service counter surface is 37 inches from the floor. Vending machine controls are positioned lower than 54 inches from the floor.

Basic Facilities

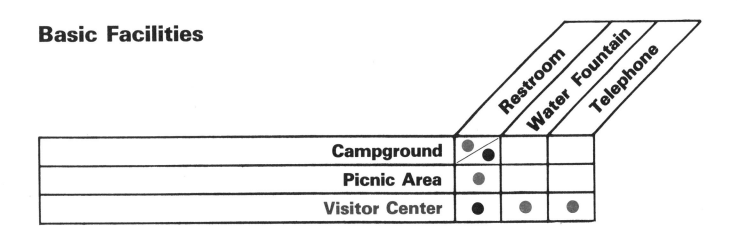

	Restroom	Water Fountain	Telephone
Campground	◐		
Picnic Area	●		
Visitor Center	●	●	●

Grand Canyon

Special Populations Coordinator
Grand Canyon N.P.
P.O. Box 129
Grand Canyon, AZ 86023
Tel. (602) 638-7769
TDD (602) 638-7772

In the Grand Canyon, geological and biological processes are combined in one awesome spectacle. The Colorado River is carving its way downward through rocks as old as two billion years. Some pieces of the geologic puzzle of what took place here still remain a mystery.

Today the Grand Canyon is about one mile deep. It ranges in width from 600 feet to 18 miles. Its length, when measured along the river, is 277 miles. The ''Grand'' and its many side canyons are bounded by high plateaus. There is a wide variety of environments here—from those at lower elevations near the river that support desert life forms, to the coniferous forests on the rims. The park may be split into three distinct areas: the South Rim, the North Rim and the Inner Canyon. Each has different facilities, activities and climates.

The Inner Canyon desert has a climatic cycle that is markedly different from the rest of the park. In March, April and May, when spring arrives on the rims, it is already summer in the Inner Canyon. Temperatures at this time of year average a high of 83° and a low of 56°F. Summer is brutally hot with average highs of over 100° and lows only in the mid-70's. Fall is the ideal time for exploring the Inner Canyon with highs in the low 80's and lows near 60°.

The South Rim slopes away from the Canyon, which funnels runoff away from the steep cliffs towering above the river. The South Rim changes with the seasons, but not all the facilities here are open all year. Snow may fall through April. When the weather is good, crowding may result from mid-May school vacations. Summers are usually very crowded.

The North Rim slopes toward the Canyon so that runoff has eroded the rim quite a distance back from the river. This area rises to more than 8000 feet above sea level; thus the climate is generally cooler and wetter than on the South Rim which is 1000 feet lower. Warm updrafts from the Inner Canyon cause spring wildflowers to bloom early on Cape Royal. Summer days are mostly clear and crisp with occasional afternoon thunderstorms. Aspens turn gold with the coming of fall when the days are pleasant and cool. Generally the best time of year to visit the Grand Canyon is in the fall. The North Rim is closed every year from mid-October to mid-May.

Climate Chart

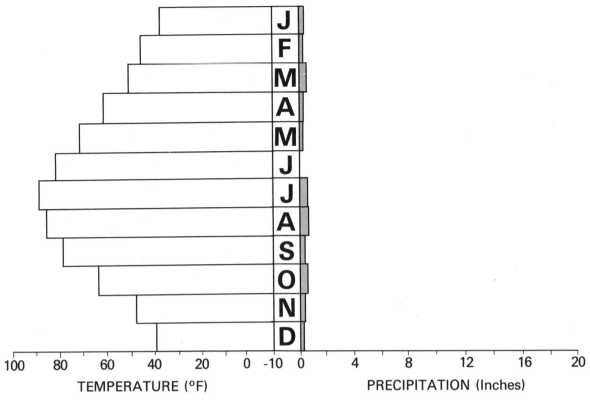

TEMPERATURE (°F)   PRECIPITATION (Inches)

Station Location: Lees Ferry, Arizona
Station Elevation: 3210 feet

Though only ten miles separate the developed areas of the two rims, the only route connecting them, by car, is a 214-mile drive.

General Information

Weather

Weather information is contained in the park introduction.

Winter Visitation

The North Rim is closed from mid-October to mid-May. Programs on the North Rim end in September. The South Rim is open for visitation during the winter. Ice and snow may make travel difficult. Winter storms bring high winds and snow or cold rain. Temperatures on the South Rim may plummet to well below freezing. In the inner canyon, January temperatures average a daytime high around 40°.

Safety

The terrain at Grand Canyon is rugged with narrow, rocky trails and steep cliffs. Visitors using wheelchairs or who have visual disabilities often need assistance. *Note: Protective walls and curbs are intermittent.*

Temperature and weather conditions can vary greatly from the rims to the inner canyon. Dress properly for the extremes in weather, take enough water and food, know your own physical limitations and seek shade or shelter if necessary.

Climbing in the canyon is dangerous. Most of the rock is too crumbly even for expert technical climbers. Swimming in the Colorado River should not be attempted. The water temperature is about 50°F year-round, and the current flows from about four miles per hour up to 14 miles per hour in some rapids.

Elevation

The South Rim is about 7000 feet above sea level. North Rim elevations

Medical and Support Services

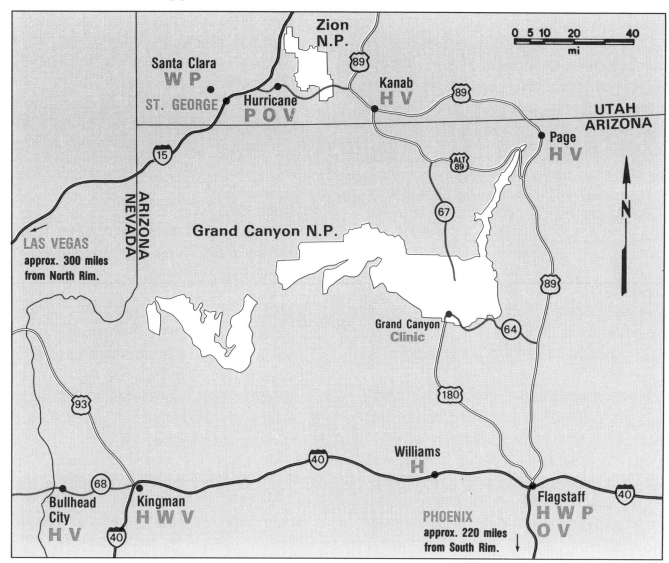

vary from about 7800 feet to 8800 feet. The air is extremely thin. This high elevation may cause problems for visitors with heart or respiratory conditions. Visitors should caution against overexertion.

Medical and Support Services

A clinic is located in the park on the South Rim. (See *Supplementary Information* section for details.) The nearest hospitals to the park are located in Kanab, Utah; Page, Arizona; and Flagstaff, Arizona, 80 miles from the South Entrance. The nearest complete range of services can be found in St. George, Utah; Las Vegas, Nevada, 200 miles west of the North Rim; and Phoenix, Arizona, 200 miles south of the South Rim.

Publications

• "Grand Canyon National Park: Access for Visitors" is a brochure which directly addresses the needs of visitors with disabilities. Currently undergoing revision, it contains approximately eight pages of access information. It is available at the entrance stations and at visitor centers or by writing to the park.

• A variety of special brochures (large-print and braille) and tape recordings are available which provide descriptions of the park and its environs, informing visitors of the physical requirements and other aspects of specific park resources. Inquire at entrance stations and visitor centers or write to the park for information.

• Descriptive cassette recordings are also available from the Arizona State Library for the Blind in Phoenix.

• "Grand Canyon Guide", the park newspaper, indicates a number of park activities and programs that are accessible to wheelchair users. It is available free of charge at visitor centers and entrance stations or by writing to the park.

• "Guide for the Disabled Rider" is a brochure that outlines requirements and safety precautions for mule rides into the Canyon. It is available at the Grand Canyon Lodge, or inquire at visitor centers.

Transportation

• All visitor areas are open to the use of private vehicles, except the West Rim which is closed to private vehicles during the summer.

• Public transportation serving the West Rim is not accessible to UFAS. Crowded conditions may make public transportation unsafe for use with a dog guide. The buses may not be equipped to accommodate visitors with particular mobility impairments. Special permits for private vehicles will be issued to visitors who cannot use public transportation along West Rim Drive. Permits are available at the Visitor Center or from the ranger at the West Rim intersection.

Sign Language Interpreter

• In recent years the park has employed a professional sign language interpreter from May through the end of October. The interpreter is skilled in ASL, wears the Park Service's "I Sign" pin and is stationed at the South Rim Visitor Center. Year-to-year employment of an interpreter is a park priority but continuity of service is dependent upon available staffing and budget.

• A sign language interpreter may be scheduled for programs at a visitor's request, if personnel and budget allow. Advanced notification is required so work schedules can be modified to meet the visitor's needs.

• American Sign Language interpretations of orientation slide program, hiking information, safety orientation and representative interpretive programs are being video taped. Visitors should inquire as to availability.

• Pre-arrangements have been made to contact a sign language interpreter in the event of an emergency.

TDD

There is a TDD available for incoming calls. The service provides pre-recorded information. A message can be left at this number for a return call. It is located at the South Rim Visitor Center desk. The number is (602) 638-7772.

Sighted Guide Method

All park interpreters are required to be trained in the Sighted Guide Method in order to provide visitors who are blind with directional and orientational assistance, if needed.

Dog Guides

Except in the Canyon itself visitors may use dog guides in their routine course of visiting park features and programs. Visitors who need to use dog guides to access the canyon proper must check at the Backcountry Office to obtain the mule schedule. Dogs cannot be on trails when mules are scheduled to pass. On the West Rim shuttle buses, crowded conditions may make public transportation unsafe for use with a dog guide (see also Transportation section).

The view from Point Imperial, North Rim.

Programs

Organized Programs

Most National Park Service facilities are reported to have accessible parking. Most paths of travel from parking areas to restrooms and many other National Park Service facilities are accessible.

Visitors should check at the visitor centers regarding access to organized programs. Some programs are accessible, or accessible with assistance. Others are held on steep, rocky trails that are inaccessible to wheelchair users. Access paths to **Mather Amphitheater** and **Yavapai Museum**, and parts of the Rim Trail (all on the South Rim) have steep grades which may require assistance for wheelchair users.

Where programs are accessible, allowances are made for wheelchairs in seating arrangements. Special programs change with the season. Visitors should contact park staff for specific details about current programs.

Brochures, fliers, signs and staff provide information about the availability and location of alternative interpretive devices for visitors with hearing disabilities. Much of the programming dependent on verbal presentation is also available in print.

Park films, slide presentations, self-guiding cassettes and exhibit message units are all available in print. Videos have been captioned.

Park staff utilize descriptive and concrete language to interpret park features. Interpretive programs may include items that can be touched. Program formats vary. Programs with potential for tactile interpretation are given at **Yavapai Museum**, **North Rim** and **Desert View**.

Arrangements for special interpretive deliveries, such as a program appropriate for visitors with mental retardation, may be possible with advance notification. Such programs are subject to available staff and budget.

North Rim

Audio-visual programs on the North Rim are given at **Grand Lodge** (auditorium may be accessible with assistance; see Visitor Centers section for details) and **North Rim Campground Amphitheater** (gravel surface will require assistance).

South Rim

• During the winter, evening programs and slide shows are conducted at the **Shrine of the Ages** auditorium. Programming at this location is reported to be accessible. Restrooms and drinking fountain inside the building are reported to be accessible.

• The **Mather Amphitheater** is accessible only with assistance because of a steep grade. Visitors should park in the upper employees area to the east of the **Visitor Center**. Entrance to the amphitheater is by a short asphalt path.

• Audio-visual orientation programs and exhibits are available at the **Visitor Center**. The Visitor Center is accessible, but restrooms are not fully accessible (see Visitor Centers section for details). Other audio-visual programs on the South Rim are available at **Shrine of the Ages** (during winter, reported accessible) and **Mather Auditorium** (assistance required).

Self-Guided Programs

The Park is expected to develop self-guiding materials in audio form in the near future. Visitors should check for availability at the **Visitor Center**, Tusayan Museum near **Desert View**, and **Yavapai Museum** on the South Rim or **Grand Lodge** on the North Rim. Materials at Visitor Center and Grand Lodge, when available, will have been tested on-site by staff and blind consultants.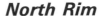

North Rim

• Vistas can be viewed from a vehicle. Curbs are present. Check with a ranger for details.

• Most locations for self-guided programs do not meet UFAS because of steep grades and narrow trails. Some areas may be accessed with assistance. The **Cape Royal** Nature Trail is flat, but narrow. It is a natural history trail. The viewpoint itself is not accessible to wheelchair users as the character of the trail changes radically in the last several yards. Accessible parking is available, but curbs may obstruct access to the trail.

South Rim

• West Rim Drive, from Grand Canyon Village to **Hermits Rest** provides several good views of the Colorado River. Accessible toilets are reported to be located at Hermits Rest.

• Accessible vistas with low stone wall barriers are located at Mather Point, West Rim and East Rim. At Mather Point there is reserved parking, and a curb cut allows access to the edge of the canyon and scenic views.

• Most locations for self-guided programs do not meet UFAS because of steep grades and narrow trails. Some areas may be accessed with assistance. Sections of the Rim Trail are potentially accessible (see Trails, below).

• The Tusayan Museum near **Desert View** features Native American programs. There is an accessible route from the parking to the museum. An accessible trail leads from the Museum completely around the Tusayan Ruin. (See Visitor Center section for details.)

• The History Room at the Bright Angel Lodge is accessible. (Entrance to the Lodge itself may not meet UFAS and may require assistance.)

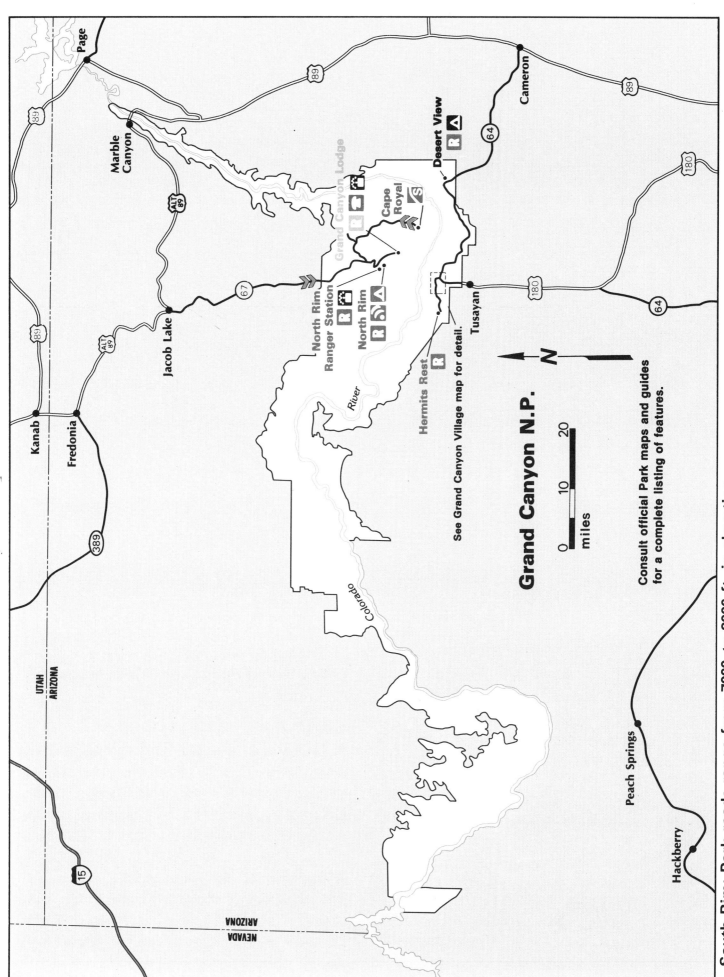

Page

Cameron

89

89

Marble
Canyon

89

ALT
89

Grand Canyon Lodge

Desert View R A

Cape
Royal S

64

180

Jacob Lake

67

North Rim
Ranger Station R

North Rim R A

River

Hermits Rest R

Tusayan

180

64

See Grand Canyon Village map for detail.

Kanab

Fredonia

ALT
89

89

UTAH
ARIZONA

389

N

Grand Canyon N.P.

miles
0   10   20

Consult official Park maps and guides
for a complete listing of features.

Colorado

15

NEVADA
ARIZONA

Peach Springs

Hackberry

South Rim: Park roads range from 7000 to 8000 ft. in elevation.
North Rim: Park roads range from just under 8000 to 8800 ft. in elevation.

Grand Canyon Village

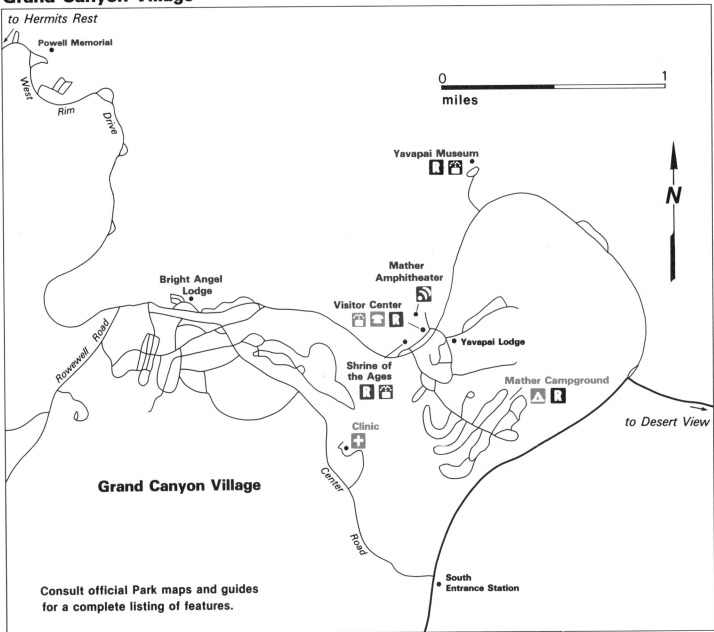

to Hermits Rest

Powell Memorial

West Rim Drive

0   1
miles

N

Yavapai Museum

Bright Angel Lodge

Mather Amphitheater

Visitor Center

Yavapai Lodge

Rowewell Road

Shrine of the Ages

Mather Campground

to Desert View

Clinic

Grand Canyon Village

Center Road

South Entrance Station

Consult official Park maps and guides for a complete listing of features.

Trails

In general, trails into the canyon are not recommended to visitors with mobility impairments. Trails are very steep and rough. There are no trails with extended grades of 5% or less.

Trails generally have signed information regarding necessary travel time.

North Rim

• Bright Angel Point Trail is not recommended for visitors with mobility impairments. Although successful use of this trail has been reported by some wheelchair users *with capable assistance*, visitors considering using this trail should check with a ranger for details and safety precautions.

South Rim

• Sections of the Rim Trail are potentially accessible. The trail features local geology. It is a narrow trail with steep grades. Hills are usually short, but assistance is required. There are a number of flat sections. The trail is paved from **Yavapai Museum** to Maricopa Point. There is a cut-off loop to shorten overall travel distance. Visitors considering using this trail should check with a ranger for details and safety precautions.

• Bright Angel Trail begins at Bright Angel Lodge. The trail is not recommended for visitors with mobility impairments. This trail is steep and rough. Sheltered rest areas are positioned approximately every 1.5 miles along trail (benches, no arm rests). Water and restrooms are not accessible to wheelchair users.

Exhibits

Many interpretive programs and exhibits throughout the park employ simple photographs and pictorial illustration which may be appropriate for visitors with mental retardation or developmental disabilities.

The accessibility of park exhibits is usually related to the exhibit's age. Newer exhibits were designed with attention to access for visitors with disabilities. Exhibit design incorporates the use of adequate and even lighting, high contrast photographs, non-glare glass with interpretive labels of high contrast.

South Rim
• The Powell Exhibit at Yavapai Point is a self-guiding exhibit that incorporates audio elements in its presentation. Information is also printed on the exhibit. Operational controls are not positioned properly for manipulation by wheelchair users. Objects are available for tactile interpretation and are positioned within reach of wheelchair users.

• At the **Yavapai Museum** a 3-D relief model depicting the "Geologic Time-Clock" may offer a tactile experience for visitors with visual disabilities. Elements of other exhibits, such as rocks, may be touched. Exhibits in a horizontal format have adjacent clear space to allow approach by wheelchair users and are positioned low for viewing. Yavapai Museum may be accessible with assistance (see Visitor Centers section for details.)

• Future exhibits with audio interpretive delivery are planned for Visitor Center, Yavapai Museum and Tusayan Museum.

Visitor Centers

North Rim

Grand Lodge and Information Center
• Includes visitor information. This facility is closed in winter.

• There is reserved, signed accessible parking about 50 feet from the Information Center. The parking area is paved, level and smooth. There is a wide passenger loading zone immediately adjacent to the Lodge and Information Center. The loading zone surface is asphalt and stone blocks.

• There is a continuous accessible route from the reserved parking to the main entrance of the Information Center. The pathway is composed of asphalt and stone blocks. Level changes less than one-half inch have been beveled.

• A wheelchair is available for loan.

• Programs presented in the Sun Room and on the porch are accessible by wheelchair lift. The auditorium entrance has five steps.

• The emergency exit is through the kitchen, with a lift to the parking area. Another exit is through the Sun Room using wheelchair lifts and ramp. This exit leaves the building, but not the area. Wheelchair lifts rely on electricity. Emergency power can be generated within five to ten minutes.

• The information desk is higher than 34 inches.

• Restrooms have been modified to be fully accessible for wheelchair users.

• The water fountain is on an accessible route. It is not placed low enough for wheelchair users. The spout allows for use of a cup and the lever moves easily.

• The public telephone is located on an accessible route. It is positioned low enough for wheelchair users, but there is not adequate space underneath to meet UFAS. It is hearing-aid compatible, but it does not have a volume control.

North Rim Ranger Station

• There is reserved, signed accessible parking about 20 feet from the ranger station. The parking area is paved, level and smooth.

• The route from the reserved parking to the main entrance of the Ranger Station is reported as accessible. The pathway is paved, but it may not be level and smooth. A ramp is in use on this route. Its grade is less than 1:12. It is equipped with handrails and an all-weather, non-slip surface.

• This facility is used mainly for information about back-country use. Hiking and camping permits are issued at this Ranger Station.

• The information desk is higher than 34 inches.

• The restrooms reported as accessible. There is reported to be a five-foot clear space in the stalls to allow for turning a wheelchair, but the stall doors do not swing outward.

• The water fountain is located on an accessible route, but it is not positioned for wheelchair users. The spout allows for use of a cup, and the lever moves easily.

• There is no public telephone at this Ranger Station.

South Rim

Grand Canyon Visitor Center

• There is reserved, signed accessible parking about 30 feet from the Visitor Center, and a passenger loading zone about 20 feet away, directly in front of the building. Accessible curb ramps are in place. The parking area and loading zone are paved, level and smooth.

• There is a flagstone patio between the parking area and the main entrance. Holes are a problem for wheelchairs. The main entrance doors are heavy to pull. However, these doors are left open during the summer. There is a side exit from the auditorium which has a ramp of 5% grade. It is equipped with handrails, edging, and an all-weather non-slip surface.

• A wheelchair is available for loan.

• The auditorium is reported to be accessible.

• The information desk is higher than 34 inches.

• Restrooms are reported to be usable. Most features meet UFAS. In both the men's and women's restrooms, the toilet stalls are less than 36 inches wide. There is not a five-foot clear space in the stall to allow turning a wheelchair. Hot water is in use at the sinks, but pipes underneath are not insulated. Faucet fittings turn easily. Mirrors are slanted for wheelchair users.

• The water fountain is accessible for a wheelchair user. The spout allows for use of a cup, and the lever moves easily.

• Public telephones are located outside the main entrance. One telephone is accessible for wheelchair users; another is hearing-aid compatible and has a volume control.

• There is a TDD available at the Visitor Center desk. It is an automatic information number. A message can be left at this number for a return call. The number is (602) 638-7772.

Yavapai Museum

• Located in Grand Canyon Village, South Rim.

• There is reserved, signed accessible parking about 300 feet from the Museum. Accessible curb cuts are in place. The parking area is paved, but there is some loose gravel.

• The route from the reserved parking to the main entrance of the Museum is not accessible to wheelchair users. The pathway is smooth pavement, but goes up a steep hill with a side slant. Assistance is probably necessary for wheelchair users. There are no steps on this route. The main entrance door is heavy.

• This Museum provides outstanding views of the Grand Canyon.

• A wheelchair is available for loan.

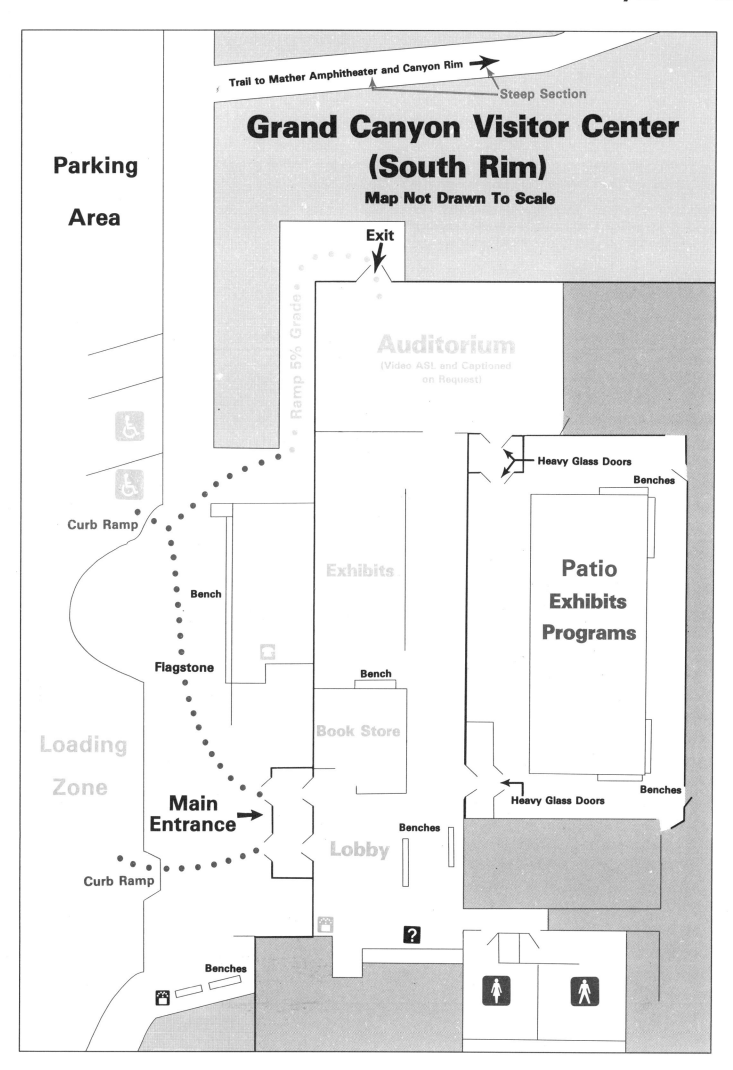

Parking Area

Trail to Mather Amphitheater and Canyon Rim

Steep Section

Grand Canyon Visitor Center (South Rim)

Map Not Drawn To Scale

Exit

Ramp 5% Grade

Auditorium
(Video ASL and Captioned on Request)

Heavy Glass Doors

Benches

Curb Ramp

Bench

Exhibits

Patio

Exhibits

Programs

Flagstone

Bench

Book Store

Loading Zone

Main Entrance

Heavy Glass Doors

Benches

Benches

Lobby

Curb Ramp

?

Benches

• The information desk is higher than 34 inches.

• The restrooms are located near the parking lot. Doorways are only 33 inches wide, and stall doors are too narrow for wheelchairs. The stalls are equipped with properly positioned grab bars.

• One water fountain is designed for wheelchair users. The spout allows for use of a cup, and the lever moves easily. This fountain is on the same level as the Museum. The steep pathway from the parking lot may be a problem. This fountain is turned off in winter.

• There is no public telephone at the Museum.

Tusayan Museum

• Located near Desert View on the South Rim along the East Rim Drive.

• There are two reserved, signed accessible parking spaces about 30 feet from the Museum. Accessible curb cuts are in place. The parking area is paved, level and smooth.

• There is a continuous accessible route from the reserved parking to the main entrance. The pathway is paved, level and smooth.

• The main exit to the Indian Ruins at the east end of the Museum is accessible. A short loop trail through a small prehistoric pueblo is reported to be accessible.

• A wheelchair is available for loan.

• The only restrooms at this Museum are portable toilets set away from the road. They are not accessible to wheelchair users. The nearest accessible toilets are at Desert View.

• There is no water fountain at this Museum.

• There is no public telephone at this Museum.

Campgrounds

North Rim

North Rim Campground

• There is designated reserved parking approximately five feet from the campsites. Most of the parking surfaces are paved; some are fairly smooth while others are broken and gravelled. The route of travel from the parking area to the campsite is over an uneven gravel surface.

• The restrooms are reported to be accessible. There is inadequate clear space in the stalls to allow turning of a wheelchair. Urinals may be too high for use by visitors in wheelchairs. Sinks are too high and have inadequate clearance to be used by visitors in wheelchairs.

• The route of travel from the campsites to the water source is not accessible to wheelchair users. The water source it is a faucet operated by knobs.

• Most cooking grills are placed at ground level. Picnic tables are present but they do not have extended tops.

• This campground is closed in winter.

South Rim

Mather Campground

• There are two regular campsites and one group site designated for visitors with disabilities. There is designated reserved parking approximately five feet from the campsites. The parking area surface is level asphalt. There is an accessible gravel route from the parking area to the campsites.

• The restrooms are not fully accessible. Stall doors are less than 36 inches wide. There is inadequate clear space in the stalls to allow turning of a wheelchair. Urinals may be too high for use by visitors in wheelchairs. Sinks may be too high with inadequate depth clearance below for use by visitors in wheelchairs.

• The water source is reported to be inaccessible to wheelchair users. It is a faucet operated by hand lever. There is inadequate clear space to allow approach by someone using a wheelchair.

• Cooking grills are reported to be fully accessible. Two of the designated sites have picnic tables accessible by wheelchair.

• Reservations are not required but are strongly recommended from May 15 through September 30. When making a reservation please indicate whether an accessible site is required. An accessible group site is also available. Reservations for this campground may be made through Ticketron®. Apply in person at any local Ticketron® office, or by mail to:

Ticketron®
Department R
401 Hackensack Ave.
Hackensack, NJ 07601

Trailer Village Campground

Trailer Village Campsites are for self-contained systems. Full hook-ups are available, however no special allowances have been made for access. Sites are generally flat. No other facilities are provided.

Desert View Campground has no campsites which are specifically designed or considered especially appropriate for visitors with disabilities.

Supplementary Information

• *Note: Some food concessions in the park have braille menus available. Visitors should inquire.*

• **Arizona River Runners** (P.O. Box 2021, Marble Canyon, AZ 86036) offers river rafting on the Colorado River through the Canyon. Published source reports: "Handicapped Facilities - Special arrangements can be made. Please inquire." No other details were furnished by the concession.

• **Babbitt's General Store** (P.O. Box 159, Grand Canyon, AZ 86023) is a retail store that sells groceries, backpacking, camping supplies, gifts and souvenirs. It includes a coffee shop/deli. It is located in the Mather Business Center, next to the Post Office and bank. Staff is experienced at serving patrons with a wide range of disabilities, including those with visual, hearing or mobility impairments, and patrons with developmental disabilities. Staff has been sensitized to the needs of customers with disabilities. No one currently on staff has sign language ability. Staff is willing to provide all necessary assistance.

Reserved, signed parking is available which is reported to meet ANSI or UFAS requirements. The parking area is paved and located 100 feet from the concession. Accessible curb cuts are present. There is a continuous, accessible route from parking to the main entrance of the concession. Changes in level between one-quarter and one-half inch are beveled. A permanent, eight-foot wide ramp is in use on the route. The ramp grade is less than 1:12. It has an all-weather, non-slip surface and three-inch edging. The deli and picnic area are reported accessible by a side door.

Aisles in the store are at least 36 inches wide and are kept free of extruding displays or inventory. Maximum shelf height is six feet. The route to the service counter is reported to be accessible. The service counter surface is positioned between 28 and 34 inches above floor, and at least one check-out aisle is 36 inches wide.

Restrooms (unisex) are located on an accessible route and are reported to meet all UFAS or ANSI requirements, except that stall doors do not swing outward.

• **Canyoneers, Inc.** (P.O. Box 2997, Flagstaff, AZ 86003) offers river rafting on the Colorado River through the Canyon.

STEVE STONE

The Inner Canyon reveals special beauty.

• **Colorado River and Trail Expeditions, Inc.** (P.O. Box 7575, Salt Lake City, UT 84107) offers river rafting on the Colorado River through the Canyon. Published source reports: "Handicapped Facilities - Special arrangements can be made. Please inquire." No other details furnished by concession.

• **Cross Tours and Explorations, Inc.** (274 W. 1400 South, Orem, UT 84058) offers river rafting on the Colorado River through the Canyon. Published source reports: "Handicapped Facilities - Special arrangements can be made. Please inquire." No other details furnished by concession.

• **Diamond River Adventures, Inc.** (P.O. Box 1316, Page AZ 86040) offers river rafting on the Colorado River through the Canyon. Published source reports: "Handicapped Facilities - Special arrangements can be made. Please inquire." No other details furnished by concession.

• **Expeditions, Inc.** (P.O. Box 755, Flagstaff, AZ 86001) offers river rafting, fishing on the Colorado River through the Canyon. Published source reports: "Handicapped Facilities - Special arrangements can be made. Please inquire." No other details furnished by concession.

• **Grand Canyon Dental Clinic** has unsigned reserved parking immediately adjacent to the clinic entrance. Parking spaces may not be extra-wide. The parking area is level, smooth asphalt. A passenger loading zone is located 50 feet from the main entrance. The route to the main entrance does not meet UFAS. Alternate (side and back) entrances are reported accessible but no particulars were furnished. Assistance may be required. Staff indicates no experience at serving patients with disabilities.

• **Grand Canyon National Park Lodges** (P.O. Box 699, Grand Canyon, AZ 86023) operates a number of lodges, with food service, in the park. Concession staff has been sensitized to the needs of guests with disabilities and has had experience serving guests with the following disabilities: mobility impairments (including wheelchair users), visual and hearing impairments, developmental disabilities (both accompanied by caregiver and unaccompanied) and special medical needs.

General assessment of suitability of lodging for wheelchair users is as follows: Most suitable: Maswik Lodge (seasonal opening), at west end of the village; less suitable: Yavapai Lodge, at east end of the village, and El Tovar Hotel, in center of the village; not suitable: Bright Angel Lodge, in center of the village.

At all facilities there is signed, reserved parking that is reported to meet standards. (A temporary parking sticker is required and is available from park rangers or at the park service operations building.) Passenger loading zones are reported to meet standards. Parking area surfaces are tarmac or concrete. Location of reserved parking is about 50 feet from entrances. Accessible curb cuts are present. If assistance is required, concession staff is "ready and willing to assist."

Slopes and ramps in use on the route to entrances may require assistance. "Most accessible" entrances to facilities are as follows: Maswik and Yavapai: main entrance; El Tovar: entrance on north end of the building; Bright Angel Lodge: lobby and restaurant are "accessible" from the Rim Trail only (restrooms and telephone are not accessible to wheelchair users). Special access routes to historic buildings are clearly marked. If necessary, staff will assist guests in entering lodges.

Guest's signature is required at registration. A clip board is available. Staff will assist with registration. Yavapai Lodge has an employee with sign language ability.

Access to rooms may not meet UFAS or ANSI. Access to rooms is over low-cut pile carpet or vinyl flooring. In all cases, the access route is at least 36 inches wide. Access routes to rooms which are external to main lodge facility are not smooth and level; assistance will be required. Where necessary, staff will assist guests in accessing rooms.

Two lodges feature rooms which have been specially modified for guests with disabilities: the El Tovar Hotel and Maswik Lodge (11 rooms). Lead time necessary for reservations may be six to eight weeks. The following description applies to these modified rooms.

The entrance door is wider than 32 inches. Two beds are present or an additional bed can be placed in the room. There is at least four feet, three inches of clear space between major furniture elements except between the bed and the wall. Locks, door handles and light switches are positioned no higher than 54 inches from the floor. The door handle is easy to operate. The mattress top is positioned about 22 inches above floor. (The bed is attached to the floor and cannot be raised for medical equipment.) The telephone does not have an amplifier but it is accessible from the bed. The alarm system is not audio-visual. No tactile warnings are in use.

In-room bathrooms have doors which permit entry by a wheelchair user. There is a five-foot clear space inside and properly positioned grab bars. The toilet is not positioned in the standard range of 17 to 19 inches from floor. Sinks are positioned properly for a wheelchair user. Hot water pipes at the sink have not been insulated. Shower facilities are in a tub which is equipped with grab bars. Tub wall height is 14 inches. Shower lacks spray unit on hose at least 60 inches long. Mirrors are lowered.

Communal bathroom or restroom facilities located elsewhere in lodges do not meet standards. There are no accessible public telephones in the lodges. Only the water fountain at Maswik Lodge is reported to be accessible.

Dining facilities are located in the Maswik Cafeteria, Yavapai Cafeteria, El Tovar Dining Room, Bright Angel Coffee Shop and the Arizona Steak House (at Bright Angel Lodge). Access is the same as to the lodges, through the lodge or hotel lobby. Arizona Steak House is accessed from Rim Trail. Assistance may be required. No information on dining facilities was furnished. Restrooms for dining facilities do not meet standards.

• **Grand Canyon Trail Rides** (P.O. Box 1638, Cedar City, UT 84720) offers mule rides into the Canyon. Trips last from one hour to a full day. Staff has been sensitized to the needs of clients with disabilities. The concession has had experience serving clients with hearing impairments, special medical needs and developmental disabilities. Groups of clients with developmental disabilities cannot be accommodated. Staff is willing to assist clients with disabilities. Participants must "be able to properly ride and control a mule safely."

• **Moki Mac River Expeditions** (P.O. Box 21242, Salt Lake City, UT 84121) offers a wide variety of motorized river trips and whitewater rafting. This concession also operates in Canyonlands N.P. See Supplementary Information under that park for detailed description.

• **OARS: Outdoor Adventure River Specialists** (P.O. Box 67, Angels Camp, CA 95222) offers rafting trips through the Canyon, from 5 to 13 days in duration. Staff has been sensitized to the needs of clients with disabilities and has had experience serving those with mobility impairments and special medical needs. Quoting from the questionnaire response, a passenger should have "strength to hang onto boat in rapids and be mobile enough to walk short distances (on sand or rock)." With special reservations, groups of clients with developmental disabilities (accompanied by caregiver) can be accommodated.

• **Outdoors Unlimited** (P.O. Box 854, Lotus, CA 95651) offers guided, whitewater trips through the Canyon. Staff has been sensitized to the needs of clients with disabilities. Concession has had experience in offering service to clients with limited mobility. Clients with other disabilities can be accommodated when accompanied by skilled personnel or a counselor.

• **Samaritan Health Service** (P.O. Box 489, Grand Canyon Clinic, Grand Canyon, AZ 86023) offers medical services to park visitors. Ample, parallel parking is reported, although it is not signed or reserved. Parking area is a smooth, level concrete surface. Curb cuts to standards are present. Passenger loading zone is similar. Both are located adjacent to the entrance. There are front and emergency entrances. Surface of route of travel is level and smooth. Ramp is in use; specifications are unreported but staff states that there has been no access problem for patients using crutches or wheelchair.

• **Ted Hatch River Expeditions** (P.O. Box 1200, Vernal UT 84078) offers whitewater rafting trips (six-and-a-half days in duration) down the Colorado River through the Canyon. Crew members have had survival training and advanced first-aid. Staff has been sensitized to the needs of clients with disabilities. No restrictions are placed on participants, but it is suggested that those with "heart problems" check with a doctor before going. Staff has had experience serving clients with a wide range of disabilities including mobility impairments (and wheelchair

users), visual and hearing impairments, developmental disabilities (accompanied by caregiver) and special medical needs. No current staff member is trained in sign language. Staff is willing to assist wherever needed.

• **Verkamp's Inc.** (P.O. Box 96, Grand Canyon, AZ 86023) is a retail store, offering Indian handicrafts, souvenirs and gifts. Staff has been sensitized to the needs of patrons with disabilities and has had experience in serving patrons with a wide range of disabilities (when accompanied by a "caregiver").

No information on parking was furnished (indicated "not applicable"). A permanent, seven-foot-wide ramp with handrails is in use on the route to store's main entrance. Ramp has an all-weather, non-slip surface. The grade does not exceed 1:12. The route is reported to be at least 36 inches wide. The store interior has a tile floor. All aisles are at least 36 inches wide and are kept free of extruding displays and inventory. Maximum height of shelves is 60 inches. Staff has expressed willingness to assist patrons with disabilities.

• **White Water River Expeditions** (P.O. Box 1269, Mariposa, CA 95338) offers "deluxe outings" (river trips into Canyon). Staff has been sensitized to the needs of clients with disabilities and has experience serving those with hearing impairments, special medical needs and developmental disabilities (accompanied by a caregiver). Currently the concession's service may restrict some clients with disabilities. (Although no explanation was given regarding the restriction, this may reflect concerns for the safety of those clients with more severe mobility impairments; this category was checked "maybe" on the questionnaire.)

Basic Facilities

	Restroom	Water Fountain	Telephone
Desert View	●		
Grand Canyon Lodge	●	●	●
Hermits Rest	●		
Mather Campground	●		
North Rim	●		
North Rim Ranger Station	●	●	
Shrine of the Ages	●	●	
Visitor Center	●	●	●
Yavapai Museum	●	●	

The view from Bright Angel Point, Grand Canyon N.P.

USGS—W.B. HAMILTON

Mesa Verde

U.S. Department of Interior
National Park Service
Mesa Verde National Park, CO 81330
Tel. (303) 529-4465

About 1300 years ago, in the extreme southwest corner of Colorado, a group of early Indians chose Mesa Verde for their home. They lived and prospered on the mesa, but near the end of the 13th century they abandoned their homes and villages. Many of their personal possessions were also left behind. Today these relics are preserved in Mesa Verde National Park.

The earliest people to live at Mesa Verde are known as the "Basket Makers" in recognition of their high level of skill in that craft. These people lived in pit houses dug into the ground:and the walls of the pit formed the walls of the house. Their houses were clustered into small villages, usually on top of the mesa. Crops of beans, corn and squash were grown. Dogs and turkeys were their only domesticated animals.

By the middle of the eighth century, descendants of the Basket Makers, known as Pueblo Indians, had begun building their houses above ground using poles and mud. By the year 1000 stone masonry began to replace pole-and-mud construction. Sturdy apartment-like

buildings were erected and by the 12th century had become exceptionally well made. Some stood as high as three stories and contained more than 50 rooms.

Near the end of the 12th century, something caused the Mesa Verde people to make another great change in their lives. They abandoned their houses on the top of the mesa and moved down into the caves on the cliffs. Many people theorize that this may have been a time of warfare and that the caves were sought out for defensive purposes.

This period of cliff dwelling lasted less than 100 years and before the end of the 13th century these people left Mesa Verde forever. It is possible they travelled south and southeast toward the Rio Grande and it is thought probable that some of the Pueblo Indians of central New Mexico today are at least partially descended from the cliff dwellers. It was not until 1874 that Two-Story Cliff House was discovered. Then, in 1906, the area became a national park and scientific excavation began on a larger scale.

The narrow, mountainous road leading onto Mesa Verde ("Green Table") has

Climate Chart

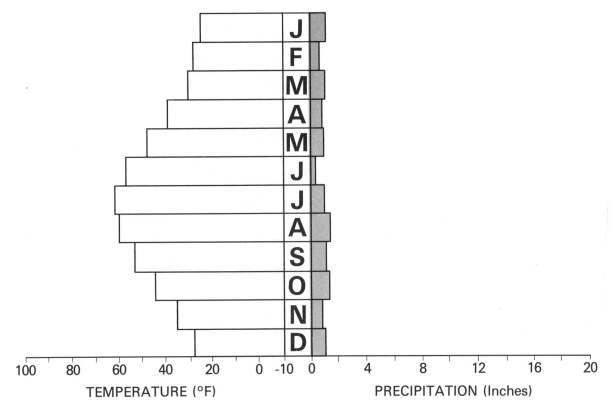

TEMPERATURE (°F)   PRECIPITATION (Inches)

Station Location: Cortez, Colorado
Station Elevation: 6177 feet

sharp curves and steep grades. There are a limited number of turnouts along the way. Travellers are encouraged to go to either the Far View Visitor Center or to the Chapin Mesa Museum first where park personnel can help plan the visit and answer questions.

General Information
Weather
Summer daytime temperatures are comfortably warm, with highs ranging from 85 to 100°F. Evenings are cool, with lows ranging from 55 to 65°. Winter highs range from 40 to 50° and lows from −25 to 15°. Snow-covered ground is normal in winter. Precipitation is generally light throughout the year.

Winter Visitation
The park is open for winter visitation. Summer and winter programming differ. Visitors should check on current programming. There is the possibility of ice and snow cover on the roads.

Safety
Visits to cliff dwellings, whether on a ranger-guided tour or a self-guided walk, tend to be quite strenuous. Often the climbing of steps and ladders is required. Adequate footwear, such as hiking boots or sturdy shoes, is recommended for these trips. With the exception of Balcony House, all major cliff dwellings can be viewed from overlooks on the canyon rims.

Elevation
Elevations range from 7000 feet at the park entrance to 8500 feet at Park Point. Strenuous activity at the high elevations of the park may adversely affect those persons who experience heart or respiratory ailments.

Medical and Support Services

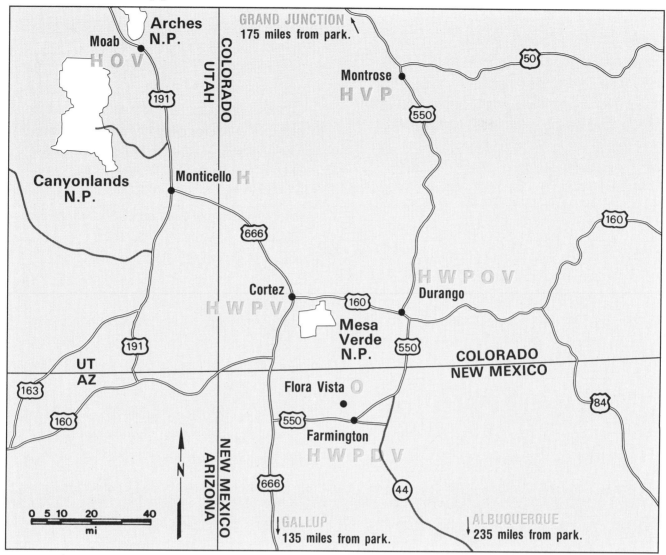

Medical and Support Services

Emergency first aid is provided at the Chief Ranger's Office at Park Headquarters and at the Morfield Ranger Station. The nearest hospitals are located in Cortez, Colorado west of the park, and Durango, east of the park. The nearest complete range of services can be found in Grand Junction 175 miles north of the park, and in Albuquerque, New Mexico, 235 miles southeast of the park.

Publications

 • "A Guide to Accessibility at Mesa Verde National Park" is a seven-page brochure addressed to visitors with mobility, hearing and visual disabilities. It is available at the Far View Visitor Center, Museum information desk, Campground Ranger Station, Chief Ranger's Office or by writing to the park.

• A braille transcription of the park brochure is available at the Far View Visitor Center and the Museum.

Transportation

• Private vehicles may be used for transportation on park roads. Restrictions apply in the Wetherill Mesa area.

• Wetherill Mesa is a distant area of the park. The 12-mile road is open only during the summer daytime hours. It is winding and mountainous, so there is a vehicle size restriction. Visitors can park in a lot near Step House. A mini-bus tour is offered beyond this point. One of the two mini-buses has been modified to be wheelchair accessible. Visitors needing the accessible bus may wish to inquire in advance at a Visitor Center to determine that day's bus schedule. Drinking fountains, comfort stations and food service are reported to be accessible.

Sign Language Interpreter

There are no park staff with sign language skills currently employed. There are no pre-arrangements to contact a sign language interpreter in the event of an emergency.

TDD

There is no TDD capability within the park.

Dog Guides

Dog guides may be used by park visitors in the routine course of visiting park features. Some ruins are accessible to dogs but those reached by ladders are not.

Programs

Organized Programs

• Audio-visual presentations are held at the **Morfield Amphitheater** (accessible but assistance may be needed) and the **Museum** Auditorium (assistance required for access). In production are a film, slide show and video tape. Upon completion these will be shown on request.

• Three videos are shown at the **Far View Visitor Center**. One shows a tour of several ruins that may not be accessible to visitors with disabilities.

• There are scripts for slide shows and all evening programs available on request. Many guide books are available which detail the park environment and describe ruin features.

• A braille script of the park brochure is available.

• Interpretive presentations sometimes include items that can be touched. Visitors should inquire for specifics.

• Orientation information is available at **Far View Visitor Center**. This building is accessible (see *Visitor Centers* section for details). A wheelchair is available for loan; check at the information desk.

• A campfire program is conducted at **Morfield Campground** each evening from early June to September. The program focuses on the archeology, history and natural history of the area. The campground amphitheater is accessible to wheelchair users but assistance may be needed. Allowances for wheelchairs have been made in the seating area. A written script is available on request.

• The **Spruce Tree House** ruin is reported to be accessible with assistance. Parking is accessible. Ranger-conducted tours are scheduled during winter. Visitors should check at the Museum or Visitor Center for current schedule. There is a trail paved with cement and asphalt, with gravel in front of the ruin. The half-mile round trip is described as strenuous with steep grades.

• A slide show at **Far View Lodge** is held on the lower level. It is accessible with difficulty; assistance is most likely required. The usual route to the main entrance involves a long, steep flight of stairs. An alternate route around the outside of the building is the only possible route for wheelchair users. Along this route loose gravel, a three-inch step and a threshold must be negotiated, so assistance is required.

• **Wetherill Mesa** is distant area of the park that is open only during the summer daytime hours. (See *Transportation* section for details.)

• **Chapin Mesa Archeological Museum** is an information center with extensive exhibits and an auditorium. A wheelchair is available for use in this area. The museum is accessible only with assistance. (See *Visitor Centers* section for details.)

Self-Guided Programs

• During the summer **Spruce Tree House** ruin is open to self-guided tours. (See Spruce Tree House in the *Organized Programs* section.)

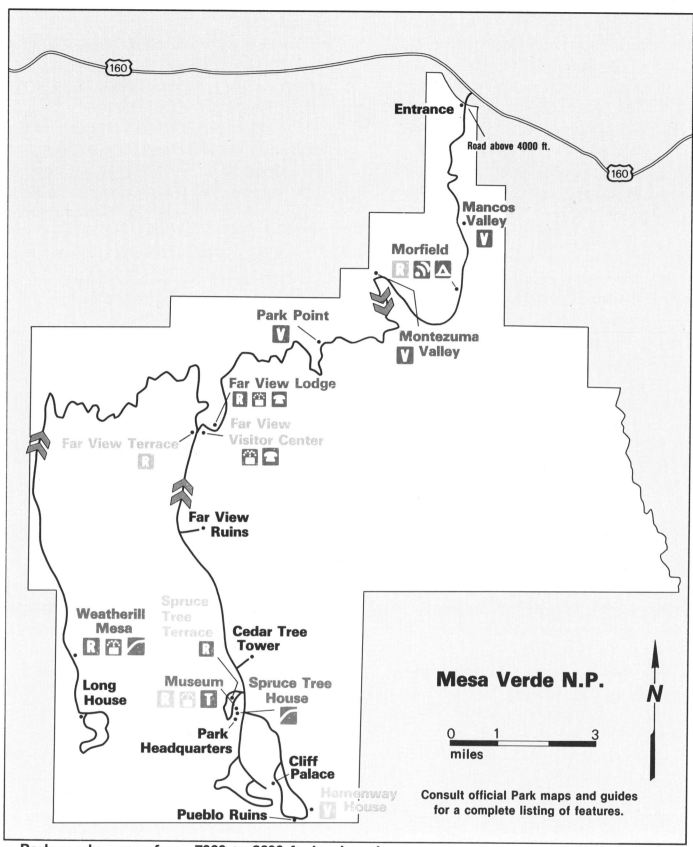

Park roads range from 7000 to 8600 ft. in elevation.

• Detailed printed information regarding park features and ruins is available at all ranger stations and bookstores.

• The picnic area on **Chapin Mesa** near the museum has sites described as accessible. Accessible restrooms and drinking fountains are located in the main parking lot.

• Ruins Road Drive/Cliff Palace Loop is a six-mile scenic loop drive. The auto tour features cliff dwellings. Hemenway House Overlook is accessible to wheelchair users. Viewing from a vehicle is possible. Check with a ranger about particulars.

• Ruins Road Drive/Mesa-Top Loop is a

six-mile scenic drive. The auto tour features a chronological sequence of the development of the native people's culture. This loop includes an excellent view of the Cliff Palace. A printed guide is available. Check with ranger for local access potential.

• Three scenic overlooks are described as accessible, with assistance needed to negotiate steep grades. These overlooks have designated parking and paved walkways. **Montezuma Valley** overlooks a fertile valley once farmed by prehistoric Indians. **Mancos Valley** provides a scenic view of the La Plata mountain range. At **Park Point**, weather permitting, four states can be viewed at once in the scenic panorama.

Trails

• A nature walk originating at **Wetherill Mesa** is accessible with assistance. Wetherill Mesa is accessible with assistance by public transportation (see *Transportation* section, above). The walk is conducted through characteristic mesa-top forest. This trail is short but its unpaved surface makes it strenuous.

• Step House Ruin originates at **Wetherill Mesa** and is described as accessible with assistance. Wetherill Mesa is accessible by private vehicle (see *Transportation* section, above). The trail passes a pit house and a cliff dwelling. Use exit-trail only. Generally the trail is paved but it is graveled in some sections and there are some steep grades. The half-mile round trip is reported to be very strenuous. Wide wheelchair tires are recommended.

• The **Spruce Tree House** ruin is reported to be accessible with assistance. Parking is accessible. There is a trail paved with cement and asphalt, with gravel in front of the ruin. The half-mile round trip is described as strenuous with steep grades; the route can be negotiated with no difficulty using a 24-volt powered wheelchair.

Exhibits

• General information is available about the park environment that is well-illustrated by photographs and other pictorial means.

• Most park signs, labels and exhibits are designed to be accessible to visitors using wheelchairs.

• A relief map of the park is accessible for viewing at the **Far View Visitor Center**. This Visitor Center also features exhibits of historic Indian jewelry, Navajo rugs, pottery and baskets.

• Book sales are reported to be in accessible locations.

Visitor Centers

Far View Visitor Center

• Elevation: 8,140 feet.

• There is reserved, signed accessible parking immediately adjacent to the Visitor Center. This can be reached by driving to the area behind the Center marked "Service Road". This area can also be used as a passenger loading zone. The parking area is concrete and asphalt and is level and smooth. This is the shortest route of entry and may be preferred by visitors using crutches: a stairway leads from this service area to the upper floor where visitor services are located. Wheelchair users or visitors with difficulty walking may wish to park here for closest access to the restrooms which are on the lower level. Along the route there is a gate but assistance from park personnel is not needed. By continuing around the building in a clockwise direction from the restrooms, the main entrance can be accessed.

• There is reserved, signed, accessible parking in the main parking area across the street from the Visitor Center. This is about 200 yards from the building. An accessible curb ramp is in place. The parking area is concrete and asphalt and is level and smooth. The route from this

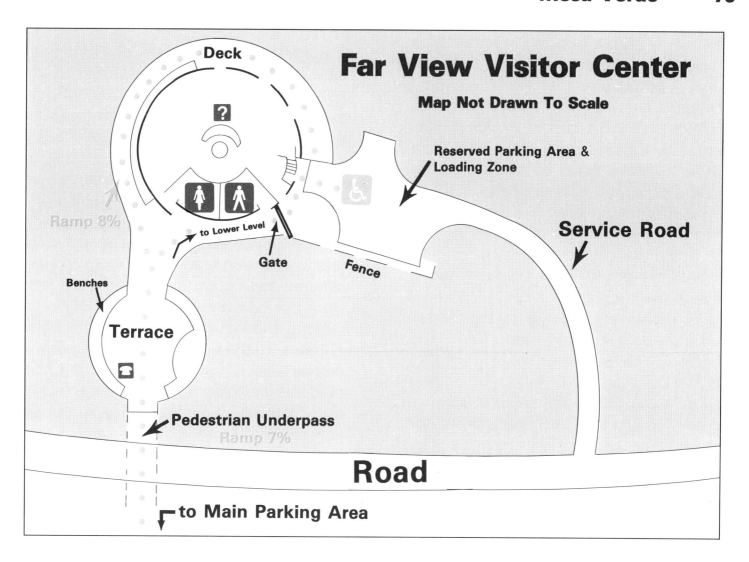

parking area to the building involves a ramp with a 7% grade at a pedestrian passage under the road. The path opens up into a terrace with seating and a telephone. From here visitors can bear right down a ramp to reach the restrooooms, or bear left on a ramp with an 8% grade to reach the deck and main entrances at the upper level. The pathway is smooth asphalt and concrete.

• Information, sales, and three interpretive videos are located on the upper level.

• There is a wheelchair available for loan. Inquire at the information desk.

• The information desk is low enough for wheelchair users but there is not adequate clearance underneath. Informational materials are placed within a 24-inch reach on the desk.

• The restrooms are located on the lower level and are accessed from the outside of the building. Park literature reports res-

trooms at Far View Visitor Center to be "accessible". These have not been evaluated in relation to UFAS.

• Park literature reports the water fountain to be "accessible". It has not been evaluated in relation to UFAS.

• Park literature reports the public telephone to be "accessible". It is positioned lower than standard telephones but may not be low enough to meet UFAS.

Chapin Mesa Archeological Museum

• There is reserved, signed parking. The reserved parking is about 100 feet from the Museum. Curb cuts are in place. These may not meet UFAS. The parking area is paved and level but there is some loose gravel on the surface.

• There is a continuous, accessible route of travel from the reserved parking spaces to the Museum's main entrance. This pathway is asphalt and cement. The

Museum is an old building built on three levels with four or five steps between them. A portable ramp is available, which park personnel move from door to door to achieve access to all the exhibits. This ramp has a grade greater than 1:12, so further assistance may be necessary. The ramp is equipped with edges.

• The information desk is positioned low enough for wheelchair users but there is not adequate clearance underneath. Informational materials are placed within a 24-inch reach on the desk.

• Restrooms are located in a separate building across the road from the Museum. The restrooms are fully accessible.

• The water fountain is accessible to wheelchair users. The spout allows for use of a cup and the lever moves easily.

• The public telephone is located on an accessible route, but it may not be positioned properly for wheelchair users. It does not have a volume control and may not be hearing-aid compatible.

Campground

Morfield Campground

• There are six designated, reserved sites. Parking is about five feet from the campsites. The parking surface is composed of gravel and is uneven. There is reported to be an accessible route of travel from the parking area to the campsite. The route consists of packed dirt and gravel.

• Restrooms near the Navajo Loop are fully accessible and all within 100 feet of the designated campsites.

• The water source is not fully accessible.

• The cooking grills and picnic tables are accessible.

Supplementary Information

•ARA Mesa Verde Company, Inc. (P.O. Box 277, Mancos, CO 81328) operates lodging, food, camping and transportation concessions in the park.

Far View Lodge offers food and lodging. The staff has been sensitized to the needs of guests with disabilities and has experience serving guests with mobility impairments and special medical needs. The lodge will accommodate groups of guests with developmental disabilities; no special reservations would be required.

There is reserved, signed parking on a smooth, level, asphalt surface located 20 feet from the concession entrance. A passenger loading zone is located 25 feet from the concession entrance. Both the parking and loading zones are accessible. Entrance to the concession is by way of a permanent, ground-level ramp with a grade of less than 1:12. The ramp has 4-inch high beveled edging. There may be abrupt level changes between one-quarter and one-half inch that are unbeveled. If assistance is required in disembarking and entering the concession, the staff will assist.

Registration is done by card with a clip board available for use. If needed, the staff will assist in registering. There is a usable route of travel between the registration desk and the rooms. The route of travel is over a permanent, ground-level ramp (as above) and a sidewalk and roadway to another building. Abrupt, unbeveled level changes between one-quarter and one-half inch may be present. If necessary, the staff will assist. The lodge has six rooms that have been specifically modified to accommodate the needs of guests with disabilities. Reservations are recommended but not required. During the busy season a one-month lead time is advisable.

The following descriptions apply to the specially modified rooms in the lodge. Each room either has two beds or can have an additional bed placed in the room. The width of the room entrance doorways is 36 inches. The rooms are arranged so that there is at least 4 feet, 3 inches between major furniture elements.

Light switches are located next to the doors and are no higher than 54 inches from the floor. Door handles and locks are positioned at appropriate heights . . . for wheelchair users and can be operated easily. The mattress tops are located approximately 22 inches from the floor. The beds are attached to the floor but cannot be raised for medical equipment. Lights above the beds are accessible from the beds but the telephones are not. There are no modifications in the room for guests with visual or hearing disabilities. An audio-visual alarm system is not in place.

The in-room bathrooms have doorways 36 inches wide which swing out. The bathrooms have interior five-foot clear spaces for maneuvering wheelchairs and have nearly all UFAS-required modifications to be termed fully accessible. This includes shower seats and 60-inch hoses with shower heads that may be used either hand-held or in a fixed position.

The food concession is located in the lodge dining room adjacent to and accessible from the lobby. The serving staff has experience serving guests with disabilities, including guests with mobility impairments (wheelchair users), developmental disabilities and special medical needs (special menu on request). Table surfaces are between 28 and 34 inches from the floor and have appropriate floor space and clearance to allow for use from a wheelchair. Access aisles are at least 36 inches wide.

Restroom facilities, both men's and women's, are located in the lobby and are reported to meet nearly all UFAS requirements, except that toilet stalls are 31 inches wide and, in the case of the men's facilities, no urinals have been lowered. The telephone and water fountain, next to the lobby, are reported to be accessible to wheelchair users.

Far View Terrace has a gift shop, souvenir shop, cafeteria and gas station. These are located one-quarter mile from the lodge. The cafeteria staff is widely experienced at serving guests with disabilities, including those with mobility impairments (wheelchair users), hearing and visual impairments, special medical needs and developmental disabilities.

There is accessible, signed, reserved parking and a passenger loading zone located 25 feet from the concession. The surface is smooth asphalt. Curb cuts to standards are present. The concession staff will assist if necessary. Access to the cafeteria is from the sidewalk. The route is at least three feet wide, has a concrete surface and is unobstructed by abrupt changes in level. A five-foot permanent ramp with a grade of less than 1:12 leads to the entrance. It is equipped with handrails, edging and an all-weather, non-slip surface. The cafeteria and the restrooms are reported to meet all UFAS or ANSI standards. The gift shop is entered from a separate entrance and it is reported to be accessible.

Morfield Village features a general store, handicrafts, gifts, snack bar, showers, laundromat, camping sites and a dumping station. The staff at all facilities expresses willingness to assist visitors with disabilities.

The store is reported to be accessible with assistance. Staff has been sensitized to the needs of patrons with disabilities and has experience serving those with mobility impairments and developmental disabilities. Accessible, signed, reserved parking and a passenger loading zone on smooth, level, paved surfaces are located 10 feet from the store entrance. Curb cuts to standards are in place. There is reported to be an accessible route of travel to the concession.

Aisles in the store are 50 inches wide and are maintained free of extruding displays and inventory. The service counter's surface is between 28 and 34 inches above the floor and the check-out aisle is

36 inches wide. Maximum height of shelves is reported to be five feet.

Restrooms in the store are located on an accessible route but do not meet UFAS; the entry doors are less than 32 inches wide. There is no 5-foot clear space and stalls may be narrow with no grab bars.

The snack bar has a patio entrance; restrooms are reported to be accessible.

The laundromat and showers are located in a separate building; each facility has a separate entrance. Shower and laundry facilities have been described as "accessible and adequate." Restrooms are reported to be accessible. No further details were furnished.

The campground (concession run) reports 15 sites with hookups. All restrooms are reported to meet UFAS.

Spruce Tree Terrace is a food concession located near the Chapin Mesa Museum. The staff has experience serving guests with disabilities, including those with mobility impairments (wheelchair users), hearing or visual disabilities ("seeing-eye dogs are welcome") and developmental disabilities ("A group

comes by bus periodically . . . the staff is prepared to assist").

Accessible, signed, reserved parking and a passenger loading zone on asphalt surfaces are located 20 feet from the concession. Curb cuts to standards are in place. The staff will assist, if necessary. Access to the concession is reported accessible over a concrete surface with no abrupt changes in level. A short, permanent ramp is in use. Its rise does not exceed 1:12. Wheelchair users may also enter the patio from the sidewalk; the first and second levels are reported accessible.

The cafeteria is reported to meet all UFAS or ANSI standards. The staff will assist. The restrooms are reported to meet all UFAS or ANSI standards, except that no urinals in the men's rooms have been lowered.

Transportation Services (interpretive tours) are offered by this concession. The staff has wide experience serving passengers with disabilities. The buses in use have no modifications or retrofittings that address passengers with disabilities but it is reported: "Our staff will assist in any way possible."

Basic Facilities

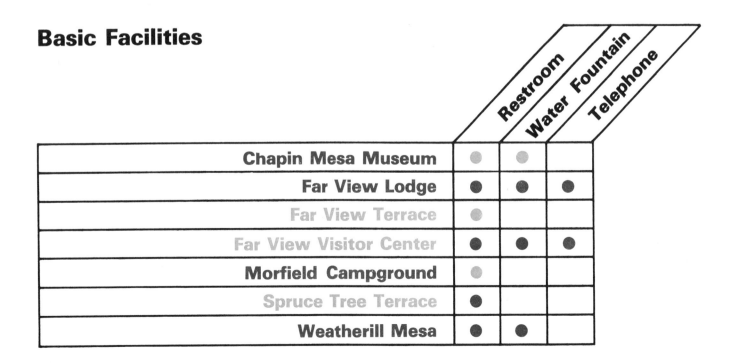

	Restroom	Water Fountain	Telephone
Chapin Mesa Museum	●	●	
Far View Lodge	●	●	●
Far View Terrace	●		
Far View Visitor Center	●	●	●
Morfield Campground	●		
Spruce Tree Terrace	●		
Weatherill Mesa	●	●	

LAURA FEASTER

A 12th century housing complex, Mesa Verde N.P.

NPS—FRED E. MANG, JR.

In Petrified Forest N.P. ancient forests are preserved in giant fossils.

Petrified Forest

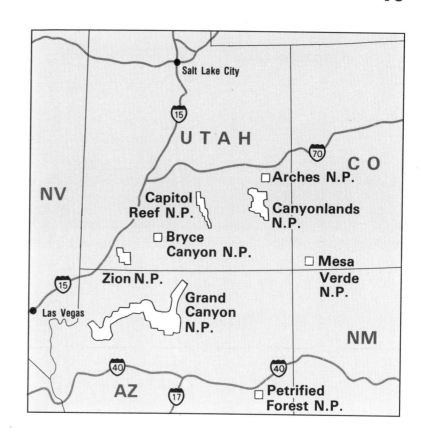

Chief Park Ranger
U.S. Dept of Interior
National Park Service
Petrified Forest N.P., AZ 86028
Tel. (602) 524-6228

Petrified Forest National Park lies in an area that was once a vast floodplain crossed by many streams. Araucarioxylon, Woodworthia and Schilderia were tall, stately pine-like trees that grew along their headwaters, south of the Park. Some of these trees eventually fell and were washed onto the floodplain. Over time they were covered by layers of silt, mud and volcanic ash. This blanket of deposits cut off oxygen and slowed decay of the wood. Gradually, silica-bearing ground waters seeped through the logs and, bit by bit, replaced the original wood tissues with silica deposits. As this process continued, the silicas hardened and the logs were preserved as petrified wood.

These events took place about 225 million years ago. In recent geologic time wind and water have worn away the gradually accumulated layers of hardened sediments, exposing the petrified logs and fossilized remains of plants and animals. Today the erosive forces of wind and water are still actively uncovering fossils and breaking down the petrified logs.

Evidence of human occupancy is readily seen on the landscape. People have used this area for more than 2000 years. Over time, a cultural transition took place from wandering families to settled agricultural villages and pueblos. Later, trading ties developed with neighboring villages. This story of early inhabitants fades around A.D. 1400.

In the mid-1800s U.S. Army surveyors came into this area and carried stories of the remarkable "Painted Desert and its trees turned to stone" back to the eastern states. In 1906 selected "forests" were set aside as Petrified Forest National Monument and in 1962 the area became Petrified Forest National Park.

General Information

Weather

Summers are dry and hot with average monthly temperatures near 80°F. Winters are moderately cold with average monthly temperatures in the 30's. Precipitation is sparse throughout the year but most of the rain falls from July through October.

Winter Visitation

The park is open to visitors during the winter season. Some facilities and programs are closed. Severe winter weather

Climate Chart

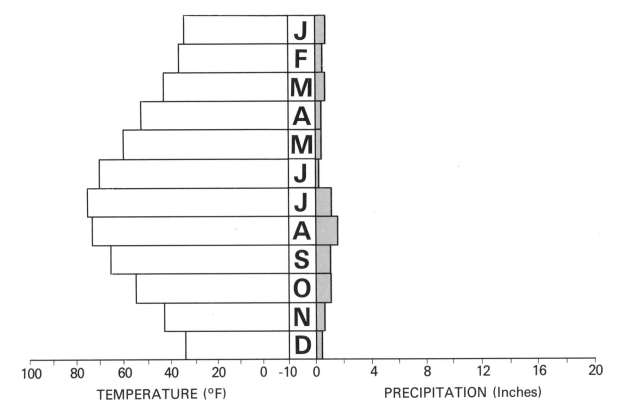

Station Location: Petrified Forest N.P.
Station Elevation: Unavailable

and attendant driving conditions may be encountered.

Elevation

The park elevation ranges from 5300 to 6200 feet. Visitors with heart or respiratory conditions should use caution against overexertion.

Medical and Support Services

The nearest hospitals are located in Holbrook and Winslow, Arizona west of the park and Gallup, New Mexico east of the park. The nearest complete range of services can be found in Gallup, New Mexico.

Publications

• ''Accessibility Petrified Forest National Park: Facilities and Points of Interest'' is a two-page outline of accessible features in the park. It is available by writing to the park.

• A large-print version and a braille ver-

sion of the park brochure, produced by Lioness Club of Fountain Hills, Arizona, are available at the Painted Desert Visitor Center and the Rainbow Forest Museum.

Transportation

Private vehicles may be used for travel on park roads. There is no public transportation in the park.

Sign Language Interpreter

There is currently one staff member skilled in sign language (ASL). Service is available at the Painted Desert Visitor Center and is geared toward orientation and information dissemination. No programs are offered using ASL. A skilled sign language interpreter may not be present every year. There are no pre-arrangements for contacting a sign language interpreter in the event of an emergency.

Medical and Support Services

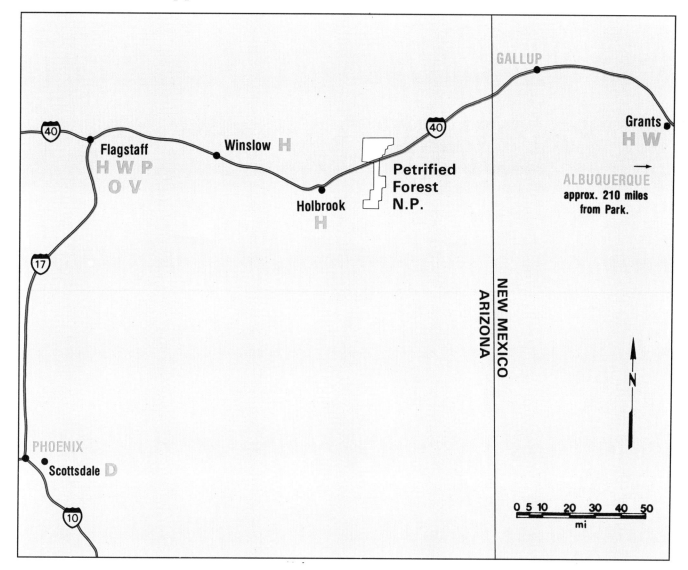

TDD

There is no TDD capability in the park.

Sighted Guide Method

There are no personnel currently on staff who have been trained in the Sighted Guide Method. At the Painted Desert Visitor Center and the at Rainbow Forest Museum staff are experienced in providing information to sighted guides.

Dog Guides

Visitors may use dog guides in the routine course of visiting park programs and features. There are no restrictions on dog guides in public places.

Programs

Organized Programs

In presentations requiring visual appreciation, park interpreters use descriptive and concrete language. There is much available for tactile interpretation, such as petrified wood or fossils. A given presentation may involve items that can be touched, depending on the location.

Program delivery makes use of simple verbal presentation, analogies and basic reasoning techniques. Programs are designed for a general audience. Staff and budget limitations preclude special arrangements for programming designed for visitors with developmental disabilities.

Except at the **Visitor Center** and

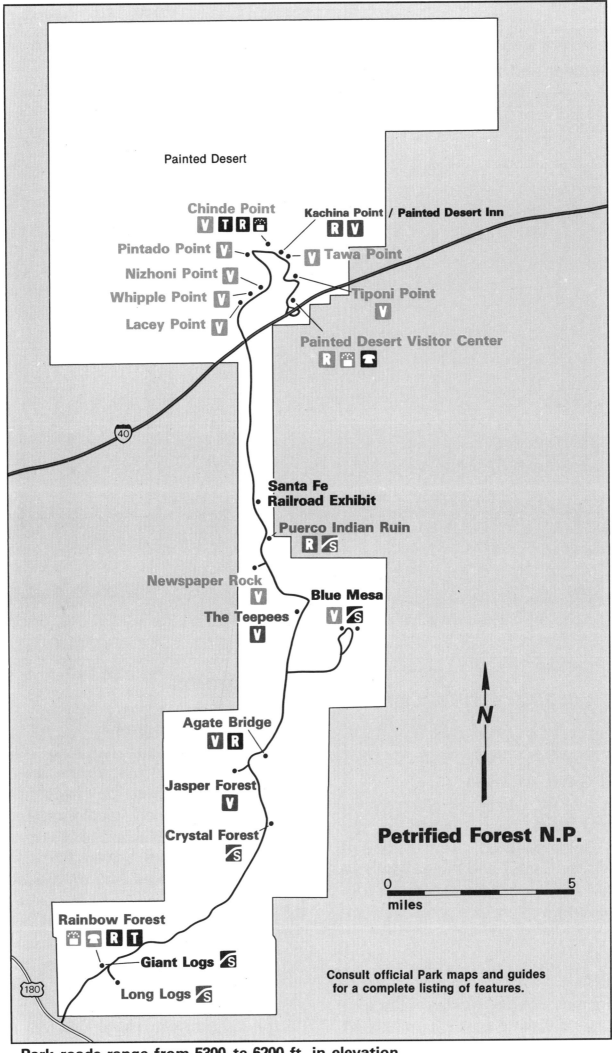

Painted Desert

Chinde Point
V T R

Kachina Point / Painted Desert Inn
R V

Pintado Point V

V Tawa Point

Nizhoni Point V

Whipple Point V

Tiponi Point
V

Lacey Point V

Painted Desert Visitor Center
R ☎

40

Santa Fe
Railroad Exhibit

Puerco Indian Ruin
R S

Newspaper Rock
V

Blue Mesa
V S

The Teepees
V

N

Agate Bridge
V R

Jasper Forest
V

Petrified Forest N.P.

Crystal Forest
S

0   5
miles

Rainbow Forest
R T

Giant Logs S

Consult official Park maps and guides
for a complete listing of features.

180

Long Logs S

Park roads range from 5300 to 6200 ft. in elevation.

Museum, there is no seating at programs. There are no special seating arrangements for wheelchair users.

• Information and orientation are offered at the **Painted Desert Visitor Center**. A 17-minute film about how wood is petrified is shown. The auditorium has wide doors, low thresholds and space for a wheelchair. A large-type, printed script of the film is available. The Visitor Center and restrooms are reported to be accessible (see *Visitor Center* section for details).

• Programming at the **Rainbow Forest Museum** includes exhibits of petrified wood and of the area's geologic and human history. The museum is accessible with assistance but the restrooms are not accessible to wheelchair users (see *Visitor Center* section for details).

• Programming may be scheduled at **Puerco Ruins, Long Logs, Giant Logs, Blue Mesa** and **Crystal Forest**. For a description of these areas, see *Trails*, below. Visitors should ask about current program locations.

Self-Guided Programs

• A series of overlooks along the park road gives panoramic views of the Painted Desert. The following overlooks offer excellent views from a vehicle: **Tiponi Point**, Unnamed Point, **Tawa Point, Chinde Point** (picnic area), **Pintado Point, Niahoni Point, Whipple Point** and **Lacey Point**.

• There are two paved pullouts that offer potential access to scenic views: the **Teepees**, a view of multicolored badland formations, and **Jasper Forest**, a superb vista of the desert floor, littered with petrified trees. There are no curb cuts, so assistance is required.

• **Newspaper Rock** is a massive rock covered by ancient petroglyphs. An overlook with a paved walk permits access to those wanting to view the petroglyphs.

• A view of **Agate Bridge** may be accessible with assistance. A short path over bedrock leads to this petrified log which

spans a 40-foot ravine. The grade of the pathway was not reported. Restrooms are located on a short down-grade adjacent to parking but they are not accessible to wheelchair users.

• **Chinde Point** Picnic Area features sheltered standard tables. Restrooms and water fountain are on an unpaved path. Restrooms do not meet UFAS.

• The picnic area at **Rainbow Forest** has sheltered standard tables. Restrooms nearby in the museum and lodge do not meet UFAS.

Trails

• Visitors may engage in self-guided tours at **Puerco Ruins, Long Logs, Giant Logs, Blue Mesa** and **Crystal Forest**. In general, full access to these areas involves use of improved trails built in the 1930s. These trails are not accessible to wheelchair users without assistance. Most areas have designated parking and ramps for access. Perhaps the areas of ''easiest'' access would be Giant Logs or Puerco Ruins but assistance would be required.

• **Giant Logs** is a 0.58-mile paved trail that begins at the side entrance of the museum. It leads up and down the hills which are covered with petrified wood. Interspersed along the trail (which may or may not be level) are single steps as well as occasional flights of steps.

• **Puerco Ruins** has no established pathways among the ruins. The paved pathway to the left of the parking lot leads to a small knoll where ruins may be viewed. The pathway to the right features two points where petroglyphs can be seen. Both pathways are negotiable by wheelchair but assistance may be required. The restrooms adjacent to the parking are accessible.

• **Long Logs** is a paved loop trail one mile long. The left path is negotiable for several hundred yards. The right side has a flight of steps to the top of a hill. A spur trail at the top leads to the Agate House ruin. A rest shelter is located on the trail. Assistance is required on all paths. Restrooms and water serving Long Logs area are located in the **Museum** one-half mile away. (See *Visitor Centers* section for accessibility.)

• **Blue Mesa** is a three-mile loop road. The one-way road leads to the trailhead. Pull-outs along the road offer scenic views. Pedestal logs are common along this route. The trail to view badland formations is three-quarters of a mile round trip. Due to a very steep incline near the beginning, it is not recommended. A rest shelter is located on the trail. The nearest facilities are four miles away.

• **Crystal Forest** trail is mostly level but has a short series of steps. This loop is 0.79 miles long and passes through many specimens of petrified logs. Assistance is required. A rest shelter is located on the trail. The nearest facilities are three miles away.

• **Kachina Point** is reached on a short rolling path from the **Painted Desert Inn**. There are scenic views of the Painted Desert. Access has not been evaluated. Assistance is likely required.

Exhibits

• **Painted Desert Inn** is an historic building with exhibits portraying park history. There is reserved parking with an adjacent curb ramp. A steep flagstone walk leads to the building. Steps into the Inn and into the display room make them inaccessible to wheelchair users without assistance. Inside, restroom facilities are reported to be accessible. (The Inn was closed for repair at the time of publication. Visitors should inquire about current status.)

• The **Santa Fe Railroad Exhibit** is not accessible to wheelchair users but a sign about the historic site can be read from the parking lot.

Visitor Centers

Painted Desert Visitor Center
• There is reserved, signed parking about 50 feet from the Visitor Center. These spaces are not extra-wide. Necessary curb cuts are in place. The parking area is paved, level and smooth.
• There is a continuous route reported to be accessible from the reserved parking to the main entrance of the Visitor Center. The pathway is paved, level and smooth. A ramp is in use on this route. Its rise is less than 1:12. It is equipped with an all-weather, non-slip surface. There are benches in the plaza outside the Visitor Center. There are double doors to enter the lobby, with low thresholds.
• The Visitor Center has a short-napped carpet.
• There is one bench inside the Visitor Center.
• The auditorium seating arrangement has space for a wheelchair.
• The information desk is higher than 34 inches. Informational materials are handed out by the person working at the desk.
• Restrooms are entered from the outside of the Visitor Center building. These restrooms are fully accessible to wheelchair users.
• The water fountain is accessible to wheelchair users. The spout allows for use of a cup and the lever moves easily.
• The public telephone is not located on an accessible route. It is outside the concession building. It is difficult to use during windy and/or cold times of the year. This telephone does not have a volume control and it may not be hearing-aid compatible.

Rainbow Forest Museum and Information Center
• There is reserved, signed accessible parking and a wide passenger loading zone about 120 feet from the Museum. The parking area and loading zone are

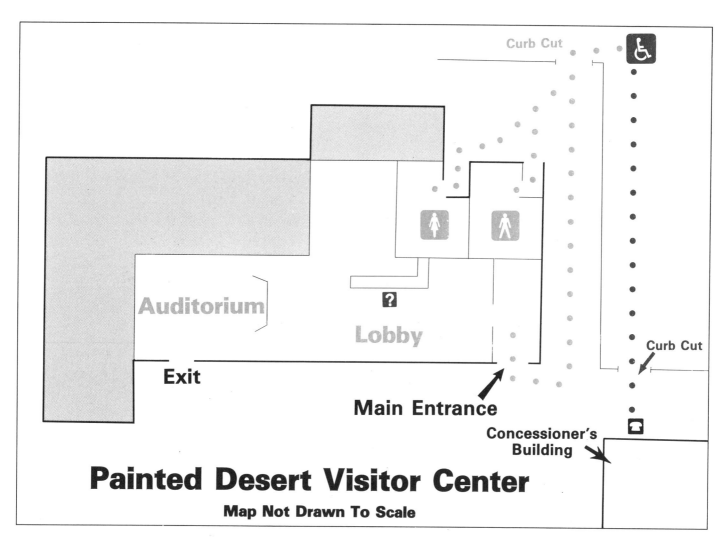

Painted Desert Visitor Center

Curb Cut

Curb Cut

Auditorium

Lobby

Exit

Main Entrance

Concessioner's Building

Map Not Drawn To Scale

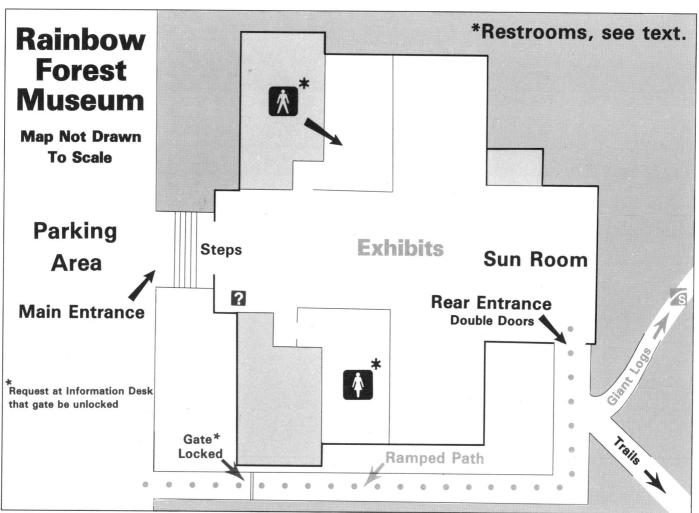

Rainbow Forest Museum

Map Not Drawn To Scale

*Restrooms, see text.

Parking Area

Steps

Exhibits

Sun Room

Main Entrance

Rear Entrance
Double Doors

* Request at Information Desk that gate be unlocked

Gate*
Locked

Ramped Path

Giant Logs

Trails

paved, level and smooth. Necessary curb ramps and cuts are present.

• There are several steps to the front entrance. There is a continuous route from the reserved parking to the back entrance of the museum which is reported to be accessible, but there is a locked gate near the front entrance. Assistance is necessary to request at the information desk that the gate be unlocked. The pathway is a paved, smooth trail. This trail is inclined but the grade is less than 1:12. The trail is equipped with edging.

• The information desk is higher than 34 inches. Informational materials are handed out by the person working at the desk.

• Restrooms are located on an accessible route but restroom doorways are only 29 inches wide. Once inside, both men's and women's restrooms are reported to be fully accessible. Faucet fittings are easy to turn.

• There is an accessible water fountain at the Museum. The spout allows for use of a cup and the lever moves easily.

• There is no public telephone at the Rainbow Forest Museum.

• There is an accessible telephone outside the Rainbow Forest Curio and Fountain concession. This telephone does not have a volume control.

Campgrounds

There are no campgrounds in Petrified Forest National Park.

Basic Facilities

	Restroom	Water Fountain	Telephone
Agate Bridge	●		
Chinde Point	●	●	
Painted Desert Inn	●		
Painted Desert Visitor Center	●	●	●
Puerco Ruins	●		
Rainbow Forest	●	●	●

Zion

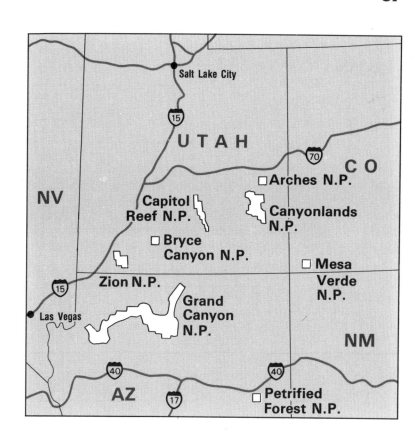

Superintendent
National Park Service
Zion National Park
Springdale, UT 84767
Tel. (801) 772-3256

In the 1800s southern Utah was a wild, rugged land of little-known canyons and plateaus. Slowly, reports and photographs spread the word that within this remote territory lay the scenic phenomenon of Zion. As was the case with Yellowstone, many refused to believe such a place existed. The passing of years saw a steady increase in visitation. Finally, in 1909, this area was added to the National Park System.

The cliff-and-canyon country of Zion is now accessible by road. Zion Canyon Scenic Drive traces the narrow, deep canyon that is the centerpiece of the park. Sheer, vividly-colored cliffs tower above as one follows along this route. The Zion-Mt. Carmel Highway was completed in 1930 and considered an engineering marvel of its time. This road crosses rough up-and-down terrain connecting lower Zion Canyon with the high plateaus to the east. Two narrow tunnels, including one just over a mile in length, were drilled and blasted through the cliffs. Two roads lead into the northwest corner of the park—Kolob Canyons Road and the Kolob Terrace Road. Both routes climb into the piñon and ponderosa pine forests of the high country plateaus of the Kolob region.

Ringtail cats, bobcats, foxes, rock squirrels and cottontail rabbits rest under rocky ledges. Mule deer seek refuge from the mid-day heat of summer under the cottonwood canopy along the Virgin River. Roadrunners, golden eagles and mountain lions also find sanctuary within the park. Wildflowers, including golden columbine and scarlet monkeyflower, are common, particularly in spring and fall.

Zion National Park is full of natural wonders such as Kolob Arch. This arch, with its span of 310 feet, is the world's largest free-standing stone arch. The narrow, steep-walled canyons, the cliffs of the plateau rim, and the strangely-shaped, colored rock formations found in Zion will awe the visitor and instill a greater appreciation of the creative powers of erosion.

General Information

Weather

From May to October temperatures usually range from 72 to 110°F in the day and from 45 to 73° at night. Brief afternoon thundershowers are common in

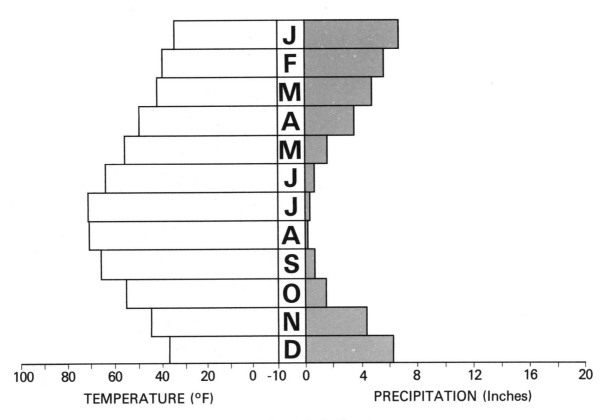

Station Location: Park Headquarters
Station Elevation: 3970 feet

July and August. Winters are moderate in Zion Canyon, with temperatures often reaching above 40°. Very little snow falls in Zion Canyon but it does accumulate on the plateaus. Spring and fall are ideal times to visit the park. During these seasons temperatures usually range from 80° in the daytime to 45° at night.

Winter Visitation

The park is open for visitation year round but services are more limited in winter than in summer. Special access camping is available in one loop of the South Campground. This campground is open only from April through October, and access for wheelchair users is not very well developed. The Watchman campground is open year round.

Safety

In summer, drink plenty of water to guard against becoming dehydrated. Use caution at overlooks and along cliff edges. Flash floods are a potential danger whenever thunderstorms are active in the area. Also be alert to the threat of lightning. Rockfalls and landslides occur frequently, although they rarely do damage.

Elevation

Elevations of the three paved roads range from 3600 to 6500 feet. Visitors with heart or respiratory problems should caution against overexertion.

Medical and Support Services

A seasonal clinic (summer) is located in Springdale, Utah two miles outside the park's south boundary.

The nearest hospital is located in St. George, 43 miles from the park. Hospitals are also located in Cedar City and Kanab. A complete range of services can be found in St. George and in Salt Lake City, 320 miles north of the park.

Medical and Support Services

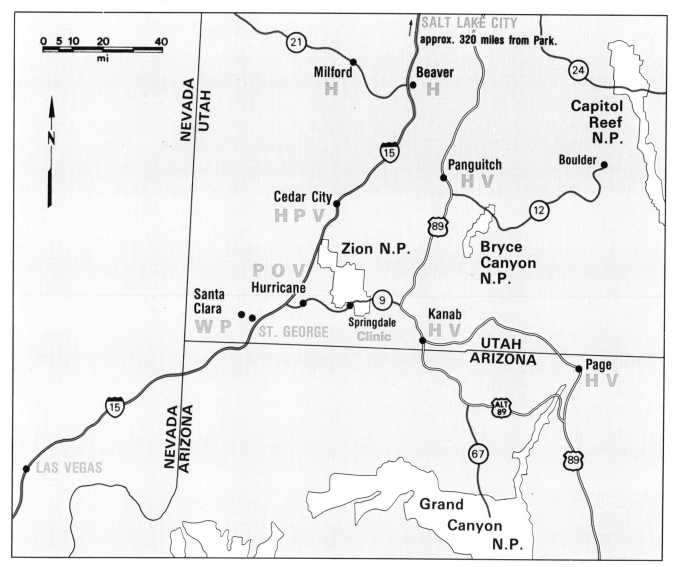

Publications

• "Access National Parks" is available for use at the Zion Canyon Visitor Center information desk. (Pages 164-165 address Zion in particular. The book was published in 1978; some information may be dated and require qualification. A revised edition is forthcoming.)

• The park brochure, "Zion", contains some information about accessible trails and campsites. Descriptions of the park environment inform visitors of physical requirements of park resources. The brochure is given to visitors at the entrance station or may be obtained by writing the park.

Transportation

All park roads are open to private vehicle use.

Sign Language Interpreter

Currently there is no park staff with sign language interpretation skills. In the past there has been staff with signing skills and future staffing is possible. The park has no pre-arrangements to contact an interpreter in the event of an emergency.

TDD

There is no TDD capability within the park.

Dog Guides

Dog guides may be used in the routine course of visiting park features and programming.

Programs

Organized Programs

Personally-led programs are conducted in locations that are either accessible or can be accessed with assistance. Programs vary, so visitors should check for current schedules.

Routine interpretation of park features may not be suitable for visitors with developmental disabilities. Appropriate presentations for such an audience may be arranged.

Verbal interpretation is available in print. There are many park brochures on a variety of subject matter from geology to wildlife. A printed script of the A-V program is available at the **Zion Canyon Visitor Center**.

• The **Zion Canyon Visitor Center** Auditorium is accessible to wheelchair users. A unisex restroom is also accessible. Audio-visual programming is presented daily in the auditorium, as well as some other programs during spring and fall. A printed script for the automatic audio-visual program is available.

• The **South Campground Amphitheater** is usable during the summer. One steep section of trail from the loop designated for visitors with disabilities might require assistance for wheelchair users. Walkways are paved, lighted and have minor grades for the most part. Restrooms and water are accessible. There are no special allowances made for wheelchair users in the seating area.

Self-Guided Programs

• Zion Canyon Scenic Drive, the Zion-Mt. Carmel Highway and the Kolob Canyons Road are open year-round. Kolob Terrace road is usually open from May to mid-November. Four roadside comfort stations are accessible. Inquire for locations.

• The **Grotto** Picnic Area has accessible unisex restroom facilities.

• A self-guided trail leads to the **Lower Emerald Pool**. (See *Trails*, below.)

• The **Gateway to the Narrows** is a one-mile-long paved trail. (See *Trails*, below.)

Trails

• Most park trails are not accessible to visitors with severe mobility impairments or to wheelchair users.

• A self-guided trail leads to the **Lower Emerald Pool**. The trail to the first pool is accessible to wheelchair users with assistance. The trailhead is located on the Zion Canyon Scenic Drive opposite the **Zion Lodge**. It ends at the waterfall above the lower pool. The trail ascends 69 feet in 0.6 miles. Extended grades do not exceed 5%; some grades run between 5% and 7%. No grade exceeds 1:12.

• The **Gateway to the Narrows** is a paved trail that follows the Virgin River upstream one mile to Zion Canyon Narrows. Ascent is 57 feet. The trail has extended grades that do not exceed 5%; some trail grades run between 5% and 7%. No grade exceeds 1:12. The trail is accessible to wheelchair users with assistance required for the last part of the trail. The trailhead is located at the Temple of Sinawava on Zion Canyon Scenic Drive. An accessible, unisex restroom is located at parking area. There are trailside exhibits. In spring and summer, hanging gardens of wildflowers are in bloom.

Exhibits

• Book sale exhibits are accessible. All displays in the lobby/sales area of **Zion Canyon Visitor Center** have been lowered.

• General information about the park is available in formats that are well illustrated by photographs or other pictorial means. Such information may be appropriate for visitors with developmental disabilities.

• Park signs, labels and exhibits are designed to be accessible to wheelchair users. Such exhibits are located at the **Zion Canyon Visitor Center** and the **Gateway to the Narrows**.

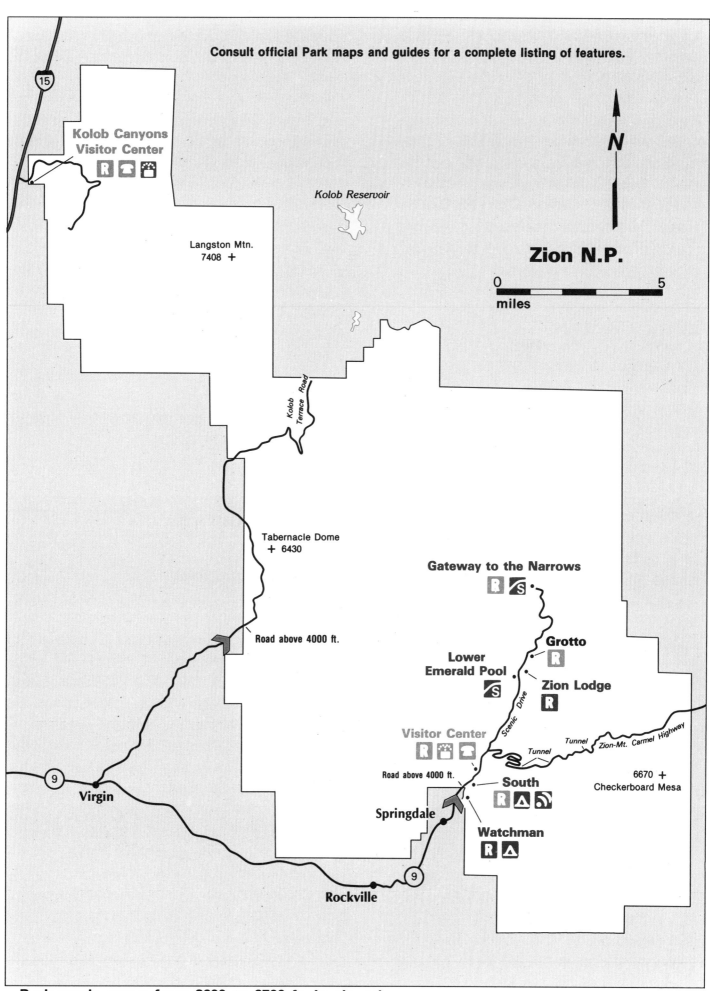

Consult official Park maps and guides for a complete listing of features.

Kolob Canyons
Visitor Center

Kolob Reservoir

Langston Mtn.
7408 +

Kolob Terrace Road

Zion N.P.

0 miles 5

Tabernacle Dome
+ 6430

Gateway to the Narrows

Road above 4000 ft.

Grotto

**Lower
Emerald Pool**

Zion Lodge

Scenic Drive

Tunnel

Tunnel Zion-Mt. Carmel Highway

Visitor Center

6670 +
Checkerboard Mesa

Road above 4000 ft.

South

Virgin

Springdale

Watchman

Rockville

Park roads range from 3600 to 6500 ft. in elevation.

• All exhibits make use of adequate, even lighting. Vertical exhibits have a reading level between 54 and 65 inches and can be approached and viewed from a wheelchair. Exhibits also have adjacent clear space to allow for approach.

• Horizontal exhibits allow for frontal approach with a minimum of 27 inches clearance from the bottom surface of the exhibit. This includes the relief model of Zion located at the **Zion Canyon Visitor Center**. This model offers an opportunity for tactile interpretation for visitors with profound visual impairment.

Visitor Centers

Zion Canyon Visitor Center

• This is the Park's main Visitor Center. It is located one mile north of the South Entrance in Zion Canyon.

• There is accessible, signed, reserved parking on a smooth, level asphalt surface. Accessible curb ramp is in place. The distance from reserved parking to the entrance is 100 feet.

• The route between the reserved parking and the entrance is accessible. It has a concrete surface and is unobstructed by abrupt level changes.

• Exhibits in the lobby/sales area have been lowered to be accessible to visitors using wheelchairs.

• The information desk is higher than 34 inches. Uniformed staff will meet visitors in front of the desk.

• The unisex restroom immediately to the right upon entering the Visitor Center is fully accessible. Two other restrooms in the Visitor Center have widened entry doors but no interior modifications.

• An accessible water fountain is located just outside the unisex restroom.

• An accessible public telephone is located just around the corner from the restrooms. It does not have a volume control and may not be hearing-aid compatible.

Kolob Canyons Visitor Center

• Reserved, signed, accessible parking is located about 50 feet from the entrance. The surface of the parking area is smooth, level asphalt.

• There is a continuous, accessible route of travel between the parking area and the entrance. It is unobstructed by abrupt changes in level.

• The information desk is higher than 34 inches. Uniformed staff will assist visitors in front of the desk.

• The restrooms are fully accessible.

• The water fountain is located on an accessible route but it may be too high to meet UFAS. The operating lever moves easily and the spout allows for use of a cup.

• An accessible public telephone is located near the main entrance. It does not have a volume control and may not be hearing-aid compatible.

Campgrounds

South Campground

• South Campground has a "Handicamping Area" with several sites specifically modified to accommodate the needs of visitors with disabilities. Sites 142, 143, 144, 145 and 146 are so-designated. Reserved, extra-wide parking on a smooth, level asphalt surface is available immediately adjacent to each campsite. Changes in level less than one-half inch have been beveled. Changes in level greater than one-half inch have been ramped. Ramps lack edging and handrails but have a grade less than 1:12.

• Restrooms are fully accessible.

• Campsites are located near a source of water that is usable but may not meet UFAS.

• Cooking grills are not at an appropriate height for wheelchair users.

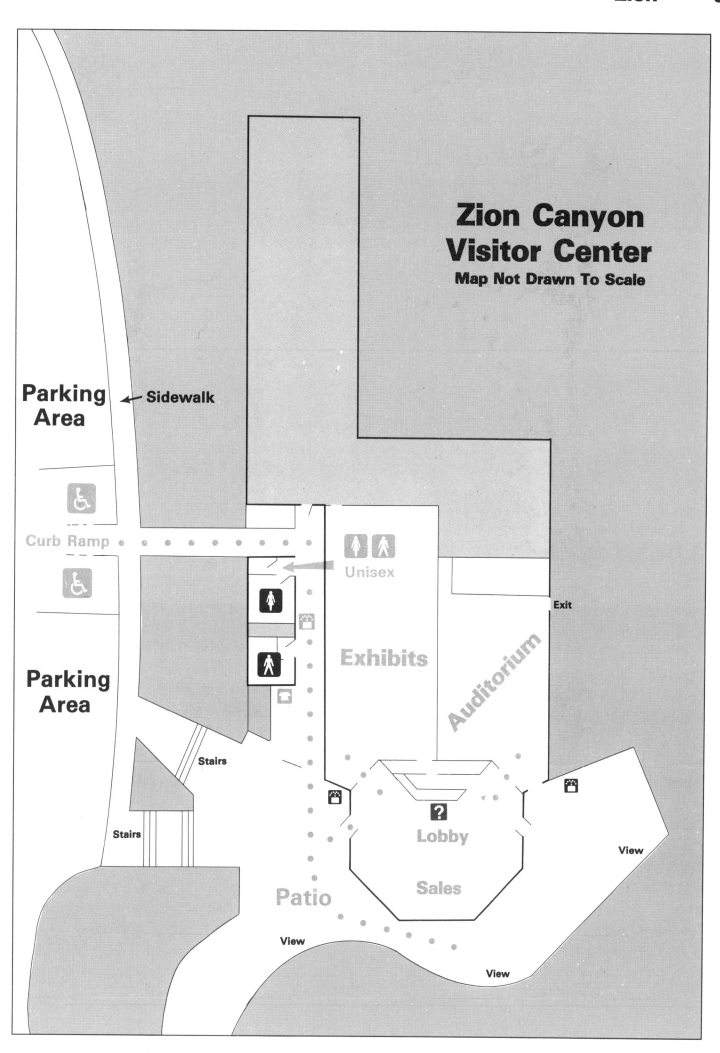

Parking Area

Sidewalk

Curb Ramp

Parking Area

Stairs

Stairs

Zion Canyon Visitor Center
Map Not Drawn To Scale

Unisex

Exit

Exhibits

Auditorium

?

Lobby

Sales

View

Patio

View

View

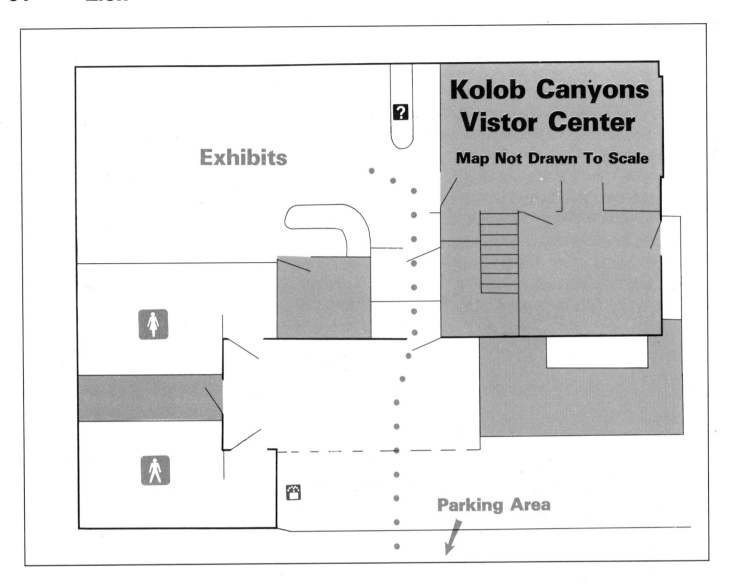

Exhibits

Kolob Canyons Vistor Center

Map Not Drawn To Scale

Parking Area

Watchman Campground
• Usable campsites are located in Loops B and C. Sites B-26, C-25 and C-29 are designated and signed. Parking is extra wide and is immediately adjacent to sites. The designated sites have a paved parking surface; others have a level gravel surface.
• There is a paved walkway to the restrooms but it may include some hard-packed gravel stretches. Abrupt changes in level greater than one-quarter inch may require assistance for wheelchair users. Restrooms have widened doors and are usable.
• The water source is usable. Drain openings exceed one-half inch.
• The grills are not at an appropriate height for wheelchair users.

Supplementary Information

• **Bryce Zion Trail Rides** (P.O. Box 58, Tropic, UT 84776) offers guided horseback trips into the park. This concession also serves Bryce Canyon N.P. See *Supplementary Information* section in that park for a detailed description.

• **Zion Lodge** (P.O. Box 440, Cedar City, UT 84720) offers lodging, food and transportation in the park. It also operates a gift shop. A published source reports the following: "Handicapped Facilities - Lodging limited. There are a couple of steps to each cabin, but lodge employees will help. Snack bar and gift shop - yes. Special reserved parking - yes, includes ramped curbs." No other details were furnished by concessionaire.

An independent evaluation done by a local disability advocate reports as follows: Parking has a hard gravel or cement surface. There is a slight slope at curb cuts. Access to the lodge is described as easy with ramp of slight grade. Corridors have no obstructions, are smoothly carpeted and wide enough for two wheelchairs to negotiate.

Rooms 101 and 102, near the motel unit entry, are good-sized. Each has one double bed. The room entry door has a threshold one-half to one inch high. It is of average weight, made of wood and glass, and operates by turn handle. Door width is 36 inches; it opens inward. Room control switches (lights, TV, temperature) are appropriately located 35 inches from the floor.

The in-room bathroom has a 36-inch wide doorway. The door does not block facilities. Space inside is adequate for turning a wheelchair around. The toilet is positioned at an average height and is flushed by a pushdown lever on the back. The sink has been lowered. Towel racks are reachable. Grab bars are present. The emergency warning system is audio and visual. Clothes hangers are reachable from a wheelchair.

In the main lodge the elevator to the dining room (one floor up) has lighted floor indicators with braille controls. Elevator controls are low. Public restrooms are reported to be accessible but the stall door cannot be closed once inside. Sink faucets are difficult to push down.

Basic Facilities

	Restroom	Water Fountain	Telephone
Gateway to the Narrows	●		
Grotto	●		
Kolob Canyon Visitor Center	●	●	●
South Campground	●		
Visitor Center	●	●	●
Watchman Campground	●		
Zion Lodge	●		

USGS—W.B. HAMILTON

Zion's scenery near the East Entrance.

Access America

Atlases and Guides to the National Parks for Visitors with Disabilities.
by Northern Cartographic

YES! Please send me the following volumes from ACCESS AMERICA:

☐ (EAST)   GUIDE TO THE EASTERN NATIONAL PARKS. . . . . $9.95 ea
☐ (ROCKY)   GUIDE TO THE ROCKY MOUNTAIN NATIONAL PARKS. . . . . $9.95 ea
☐ (WESTER)   GUIDE TO THE WESTERN NATIONAL PARKS . . . . $10.95 ea
☐ (SOUTHW)   GUIDE TO THE SOUTHWESTERN NATIONAL PARKS . . . . $10.95 ea

☐ I have enclosed a check or money order for the cost of the books, plus $1.50 for postage and handling (add 75¢ for each additional copy). I have enclosed $_____

☐ Please charge my VISA/MasterCard/ American Express (circle one) card account.

     Card Number _____

     Expiration Date _____

     Signature _____

SOURCE CODE: AAPS

NAME _____

ADDRESS _____ APT. ____

CITY _____ STATE ___ ZIP ___

TELEPHONE NUMBER _____

(For multiple copies to different addresses, please list on separate sheet.)

For groups interested in bulk sales, contact: Weidenfeld & Nicolson, Special Sales Department (212) 614-7936.

Access America

Atlases and Guides to the National Parks for Visitors with Disabilities.
by Northern Cartographic

YES! Please send me the following volumes from ACCESS AMERICA:

☐ (EAST)   GUIDE TO THE EASTERN NATIONAL PARKS. . . . . $9.95 ea
☐ (ROCKY)   GUIDE TO THE ROCKY MOUNTAIN NATIONAL PARKS. . . . . $9.95 ea
☐ (WESTER)   GUIDE TO THE WESTERN NATIONAL PARKS . . . . $10.95 ea
☐ (SOUTHW)   GUIDE TO THE SOUTHWESTERN NATIONAL PARKS . . . . $10.95 ea

☐ I have enclosed a check or money order for the cost of the books, plus $1.50 for postage and handling (add 75¢ for each additional copy). I have enclosed $_____

☐ Please charge my VISA/MasterCard/ American Express (circle one) card account.

     Card Number _____

     Expiration Date _____

     Signature _____

SOURCE CODE: AAPS

NAME _____

ADDRESS _____ APT. ____

CITY _____ STATE ___ ZIP ___

TELEPHONE NUMBER _____

(For multiple copies to different addresses, please list on separate sheet.)

For groups interested in bulk sales, contact: Weidenfeld & Nicolson, Special Sales Department (212) 614-7936.

Access America

Atlases and Guides to the National Parks for Visitors with Disabilities.
by Northern Cartographic

YES! Please send me the following volumes from ACCESS AMERICA:

☐ (EAST)   GUIDE TO THE EASTERN NATIONAL PARKS. . . . . $9.95 ea
☐ (ROCKY)   GUIDE TO THE ROCKY MOUNTAIN NATIONAL PARKS. . . . . $9.95 ea
☐ (WESTER)   GUIDE TO THE WESTERN NATIONAL PARKS . . . . $10.95 ea
☐ (SOUTHW)   GUIDE TO THE SOUTHWESTERN NATIONAL PARKS . . . . $10.95 ea

☐ I have enclosed a check or money order for the cost of the books, plus $1.50 for postage and handling (add 75¢ for each additional copy). I have enclosed $_____.

☐ Please charge my VISA/MasterCard/ American Express (circle one) card account.

     Card Number _____

     Expiration Date _____

     Signature _____

SOURCE CODE: AAPS

NAME _____

ADDRESS _____ APT. ____

CITY _____ STATE ___ ZIP ___

TELEPHONE NUMBER _____

(For multiple copies to different addresses, please list on separate sheet.)

For groups interested in bulk sales, contact: Weidenfeld & Nicolson, Special Sales Department (212) 614-7936.

BUSINESS REPLY MAIL

FIRST CLASS   PERMIT NO. 2181   NEW YORK, N.Y.

POSTAGE WILL BE PAID BY ADDRESSEE

WEIDENFELD & NICOLSON NY / GROVE PRESS
SALES DEPARTMENT
841 BROADWAY
NEW YORK, NY 10211-0185

BUSINESS REPLY MAIL

FIRST CLASS   PERMIT NO. 2181   NEW YORK, N.Y.

POSTAGE WILL BE PAID BY ADDRESSEE

WEIDENFELD & NICOLSON NY / GROVE PRESS
SALES DEPARTMENT
841 BROADWAY
NEW YORK, NY 10211-0185

BUSINESS REPLY MAIL

FIRST CLASS   PERMIT NO. 2181   NEW YORK, N.Y.

POSTAGE WILL BE PAID BY ADDRESSEE

WEIDENFELD & NICOLSON NY / GROVE PRESS
SALES DEPARTMENT
841 BROADWAY
NEW YORK, NY 10211-0185